LIFTING THE VEIL

A FAIRIE TALE

PHILIP J. GRIMM

authorHOUSE®

AuthorHouse™
1663 Liberty Drive
Bloomington, IN 47403
www.authorhouse.com
Phone: 1 (800) 839-8640

Published by AuthorHouse 11/24/2015

ISBN: 978-1-5049-6461-6 (sc)
ISBN: 978-1-5049-6462-3 (hc)
ISBN: 978-1-5049-6460-9(e)

Library of Congress Control Number: 2015919642

Print information available on the last page.

CONTENTS

PREFACE

This book is unlike anything you have ever read. It is unique; it goes many places and does many things. It gets out into the weeds and appears to get lost. It circles, changes subjects, concentrates on trivia, and then suddenly transforms itself into a hermeneutic. The body of hermeneutic literature is rather small. In fact, you may be holding the only new hermeneutical book written within the last two hundred years.

Hermeneutics is an awkward word. It does not sit well on the English ear. It sounds like it was created during a barroom brawl of eighteenth-century German philosophers. It is a study of alternative ways to interpret the canon of holy literature. Mostly, it has been used to describe the varieties of Protestant beliefs created during the Reformation.

This book is based upon one simple thought: the human soul is a real creature. It can be identified and measured, and its behavior can be predicted. The human soul is neither a metaphysical entity nor a metaphor. The human soul is the intended reader of the holy Canon, even though the soul is never mentioned within the holy literature. The Bible is a teaching instrument informing the human soul how to be a successful human being.

The story is told as if it were a fairy tale. Fairy tales do not have to start with the words "once upon a time." Nor do they have to end with the words "and everyone lived happily ever after." Fairy tales are the poor man's version of holy literature. Each tale is intended to teach a lesson about some important aspect of being human. Fairy tales convey an ultimate truth while lying, embellishing, obfuscating, and otherwise coloring the described events. Not all fairy tales are successful. Some tales are easy to tell, other tales are easy to understand, and still other tales just get confusing. A fairy tale does not have to be true. All that matters is that it *could* be true, and the strength of the tale depends upon how much the teller of the tale believes the story to be true.

I put myself into this tale because I had to. There is no way to say these things without having someone to say them. I am a died-in-the-wool secularist who grew up on the hedonistic shores of Southern California. I'm an aging, modern American who started life with a few discordant memories, but whose religion was sex, drugs, and rock and roll. Religion was for those too stupid to recognize the real world.

And then I was proven wrong. All religious experiences are personally convincing, but they require interpretation. It is during the interpretation process that religious messages become distorted. In order to tell this story, I had to intentionally distort the message by turning myself into a talented cosmic superhero, which was good for the ego but was an obvious exaggeration, if not an outright lie.

But these foibles only serve to strengthen the story and move the narrative. I swear upon my dead grandmother Grimm's grave that the story you are about to read is both true and important. And if you can see your way past the jargon, it is a good story.

1

THE LIBRARIANS

The true nature of humanity remains a mystery, even after fifteen thousand years. There are many possible explanations for this. The current most popular theory for this mystery is that we evolved from the apes and that *Homo sapiens* is a hard animal to understand. Modern science is only now gaining the tools necessary to anatomically, biochemically, and physiologically dissect the *Homo sapiens* brain, and it takes time to interpret the information we are discovering. Understanding the functionality of the *Homo sapiens* brain is hard. It is hard to understand what is happening in the brain, and it is even harder to understand why.

A second reason why the workings of the human being remain a mystery is that much of what happens with the human being is happening on a level not recognized by human consciousness. This is clearly evident when dealing with things like homeostasis—body heat, heart rate, breathing, and blood sugar levels—as the human does not consciously control any of these things. Though the parameters are less clear, we also have little or no conscious control over appetite, sexual attraction, or emotions. But we humans convince ourselves that we have complete conscious control over the important things in life, things like our jobs, our marriages, and our money. Indeed the secularists believe that the only valid decisions a human being makes are those that arise from conscious, rational thought.

But the truth is stranger than that. As we will see, the human being did not just evolve from the ape. God manipulated *Homo sapiens* and then conjoined His (or Her or Its) children with *Homo sapiens*, an artificial act that tethered the human soul to *Homo sapiens* and created the human being. As will become obvious during this story, there is not sexual gender assigned to God.

The human being is clearly different from and more talented than any other animal on earth. Why we are different from all the rest of the animals is the mystery that is not yet answered to anyone's satisfaction. There is an easy explanation for why this is so: there are no reliable and recognizable channels of communication between the human being and heaven. We will find that this is perhaps God's biggest mistake. He used the wrong host animal to carry and protect His children. He used a host animal that did not have the memory banks to consciously remember or interpret the content of its dreams.

It was through the dreaming process that God had intended to communicate with His children. The fact that using this host animal was a mistake was apparent within the first twenty years of the conjoining of the human soul with *Homo sapiens*, an act that occurred about fifteen thousand years ago, just shortly after the last ice age. The resultant behavior of the human being has been a disappointment, and God has been continuously hounded by critics to end this commitment to the human. God's rationale for not turning His back upon humanity is that the children who survive this brutal childhood are honed to a fine edge and become exemplary adults.

To compensate for the lack of communication between parent and child, God has had to jury-rig a system for explaining things to the human being. It is not an efficient system, and it is subject to gross distortions and miscommunication. It is surprising that it works as well as it does, and it does work.

God is a member of the species *Humanitas eternitas*. All of the adults of this specie live in heaven, and all of their children live on earth. There are twenty-six subtypes of *Humanitas eternitas*, and most members of this specie belong to just twelve of the twenty-six. There is a rare subtype of *Humanitas eternitas*, which we will call "the Librarians." This subtype makes up less than one one-hundredth of one percent of the *Humanitas eternitas*, but these individuals have certain genetic skills that God has employed to communicate with His children on earth. They can remember things, and if they cannot remember an answer, they can intuit things that others cannot. They have a separate skill qualifying them as empaths. In short, they know where and how to find the answer.

In the early days of humanity, ten to fifteen thousand years ago, there were fewer than one hundred of these Librarians wandering the earth, but as the human soul population on earth expanded, so did the number of Librarians. There are now about two thousand Librarians on earth. Each of these two thousand individuals were specially trained in a place called Valhalla, an intermediary place located between heaven and earth where human souls are gathered for rest and relaxation between their sojourns on earth. The goal of the Librarians is to serve as the outsiders who push, pull, cajole, or otherwise manipulate the consciousness of humanity in the direction God desires. Like I said, this is not an effective way to supervise children. The results are spotty.

When they arrived on earth, none of these two thousand possessed a mark of authority, and their training did not guarantee infallibility. Most Librarians end up on the razor's edge that separates genius from insanity. Most of these individuals fail in their mission to shape the course of human history, and God spends a lot of time giving pep talks and encouragement to them when they return to Valhalla. But sometimes things happen the way they should. Sometimes the Librarians are successful; sometimes humanity stops before the brink; and sometimes humanity turns in the right direction.

I am one of the Librarians. I do not say this in a boastful way but in more of an "outcast" way. I have not always been the outsider, but I've always been brittle and brilliant in battle. I was not the best choice for dependability and social interaction, as I was smart enough but alienating. For this particular encounter with life on earth, I was called upon because I was simply available; no other special trait was required.

The one I believe to be God took me out of sequence, and I was escorted to Him in the first hour that I awoke from my previous lifetime—with memories of my previous *Homo sapiens* host animal fresh in my mind. Something catastrophic had happened. God was upset. A plan He had been working on had failed catastrophically. The group of Librarians He had counted on to perform in one way had chosen to go in a different direction, and catastrophe had occurred.

It was 1951, the year one of my host animals died and my current host animal was born. It usually takes longer to transit—like *years* longer. You can spend a lot of time hanging out in little cells in Valhalla while you wait for the next potential host animal to be born. It can be boring in the way station when you are really young, but as you progress through the instars, you get to hang out with a lot of great people who know you and have heard all your stories about the weird or appalling ways you've died. So, while it is fun to hang out in Valhalla, you cannot spend your whole life there. You have to molt, and that means you have to go and live with another host animal for a while. Being put into direct confinement within a *Homo sapiens* is fun in a miserable way.

So, God did not let me get enough sleep before He called me to ask me to do something very difficult. He asked me to endure a *Homo sapiens* pregnancy as its fetus, but to do it without benefit of receiving the deep, sleep-inducing week of the serotonin spike. This would mean that I would retain memories of some scattered events that had occurred either in Valhalla on previous returns or during my more recent incarnations. And then He made me promise to tell as many people as I could, as much as I could remember of those events.

God was frightened because humanity had exploded two atomic bombs during an act of war, and now the Soviets were getting the bomb, and most of the human souls currently living on earth were suddenly vulnerable to a previously unimagined energy source. Religious lunatics were going to annihilate mature instars before they could perform their transcendence. God was uncomfortable and feared for His children. Two major mileposts had been missed in the last two hundred years. Secularism was a mistake. He was thinking of pulling the plug on humanity and not sending any more souls into the world.

God said that He had to send a message to humanity and that I was the only one currently available to take it. He gave me the option of five different fetuses, but He had preselected one as the best of several bad choices. In a matter of days I was back in a womb, and I did not like it. Neither did I like it when I was born. I refused to eat. I was born at seven pounds, and at three months I weighed five. I did enjoy my little peepee. I entered life as a child knowing more and recognizing more than either of my parents. I was a little shit.

But I had memories. I *really* remembered standing in front of an amazing, gentle man with a sad smile, promising that I would reveal to as many people as possible all of the memories I'd retained. Early on, it was a cheap promise, and the reason I could not fulfill the promise was that when I remembered it, I could not write it down, and when I could write it down, I could not remember it. The memory sounded contrived, and for a long time it lacked context, but this memory was the barrier that stood between me and the rest of the world for most of my life. It certainly got in the way between me and the mother of my children. For most of my life I was tortured by memories I could not understand.

Until 2005. My host animal and I were doing our forty-five-minute commute to and from work, listening to a Teaching Company course about the history of science in the twentieth century, when I suddenly had an epiphany about where heaven was, what it was like, and the nature of time. That burst of knowledge unleashed an avalanche of knowledge. I recoiled and absorbed this access to the knowledge of the universe, and I realized that any question I could frame would be answered. So I asked a few questions. And I took copious notes. I've talked with a shrink about it, and he thinks I had a manic fugue. With all due respect to psychiatry, I think it was a religious experience similar to those described in parts of William James's *The Varieties of Religious Experience*. But I think I also found other areas of similarity in my normal thinking process when I read William James's *Textbook of Psychology*. I found comfort in reading those books. William James was a Librarian.

Unfortunately, this religious experience of 2005 meant that God had called my bluff. He provided me with enough context to understand. I did not know He could do interventional stuff, like the second episode I endured in the autumn of 2005. He was behind it, but I did not see Him during the event. But now, as a result of this second religious experience, I no longer had the excuse of not remembering that which God had asked me to speak about.

I remembered Valhalla, or at least I remembered the classrooms, the lecture halls, the group discussions, and the reading of old books. I remember cells li ning some of the walls, filled with immature instars, each infant in a small prison cell. But I also remember watching them be released from their cells and their running around like wild animals. I remember a few special people and a few special moments. And I remember walking up onto a stage where a machine that looked like a refrigerator-sized microscope was aiming at my new home, and I had to bow my neck into the beam. Not a lot of fun. When it was over, I found myself alone, wet, and in the dark, and I cried myself to sleep.

I remember, and have always remembered, one more detail. As I stood there before the machine that was going to conjoin me to another *Homo sapiens*, I asked Him whom I regard as God, "How am I to perform this public proclamation of the stagecraft behind humanity?" His response was, "Take advantage of your new name. You have carried this name before, and one reason I have chosen this host animal for you is because of his name. Call your story a fairy tale."

It has taken me ten years since my religious experience to assimilate that which I was exposed to. The first milestone in my epiphany was the realization that the human soul is real, that it is not a metaphor. In fact, the you that is you—the one who is reading this book—is the human soul. The *Homo sapiens* is the animal holding the book. There is a big difference there. The *Homo sapiens* is not the human being.

Let's return to the Librarians. Historically they have been sent to earth as male members of the *Homo sapiens* specie, but that is a bow to the intolerance of the human community on earth, not a reflection of God's preference for men. Until recently, the female *Homo sapiens* was ignored or actively suppressed by human society. In the early days of humanity, each Librarian sent to earth had knowledge and skills far above the average human being. The results were unfortunate; their fellow human beings recognized the Librarians as special and often elevated them to the status of demigods. Worse yet, the Librarians themselves came to believe that they were demigods. Early on, the Librarians did more harm to God's cause than good. Gilgamesh and his buddy Enkidu were Librarians. Hammurabi was a Librarian. Much later, Abraham was a Librarian.

As the intelligence and sophistication of the human community grew, the distinction between a Librarian and a regular human being became less obvious, and at this current point in time, there is really no distinction between regular people and the Librarians.

As a result, the Librarians have faded into the woodwork. God changed strategies, and after 1000 CE, few, if any, Librarians were sent to earth to discuss God or religion. Instead they were talking about topics like mathematics, physics, philosophy, chemistry, and human governance, just to name a few. Like I said, these Librarians remember stuff. They spend their tenure here on earth concentrating upon a single point of human potential, and then they try to imbed that knowledge or skill into the human psyche. Perhaps the ideas they introduce will not be embedded as deeply as archetypes are embedded into the human psyche, but they leave an intent. It is best if we do not delve too deeply into the romantic German philosophers.

Though the Librarians are scattered throughout the population, these scatterings were not random, *ad hoc* events throughout history. Rather, the Librarians came in waves, like seeds being sowed in a field. Usually the Librarians came in groups of two or three. Sometimes they came in groups of thirty or forty. The subject matter of their individual goals has changed over time, for humanity has proven resistant to the Librarians' talking about the subject of God and religion. Therefore, during the last millennia, God has tended to concentrate on other areas of human thought.

Everyone, not just the Librarians, is stuck here on earth. We do not have a choice. Most of us do not even recognize an alternative to our current life, and the Librarians are the same. The Librarians do not realize that they are unique, so how do they make their lives work? How does one recognize an absolute? How does one recognize a discrete variable? What are the boundaries of life? Is it possible to lift the edge of human life and look under the covers? How do these Librarians remember what they remember? In part, they remember because of poorly understood human traits: intuition and the similar but separate skill of empathy.

Many people can intuit the thoughts, motives, and previous histories of others. This is a common skill that is poorly understood. Other people can remember events from a previous human life, while still others can understand and share emotions that people try to hide. These skills are neither good nor evil, and much information discovered through intuition and empathy is hidden from public view. It is through these intuitions, half-remembered thoughts, and pursuit of the unconscious part of humanity that contact with heaven is made. This contact is open to everyone, not just the Librarians.

The Librarians have two particular talents in this nonrational area of human thought, and we call them *intuition* and *empathy*. Librarians can sift through the confusion and fear associated with heavenly contact. They can find and collect the odd truths that can be converted into a human understanding of earth. This is not an easy process; it can take years to assimilate these fragments of knowledge. The Librarians were never intended to have happy lives, to live in comfort, or to be pillars of society. They were the eccentric, odd, talented outsiders. They were intended to steer society, like a rudder steers a ship.

God did not have to teach the human to speak; that came spontaneously when the human soul was introduced into the *Homo sapiens*. But God spent millennia and much energy teaching humanity the concept of a written language, the concept of numbers, and the power of mathematics. He thought the first few steps the human would take to separate itself from the *Homo sapiens* would be the hardest, but that has not proven to be the case. Humanity has proven resistant to instruction or supervision.

The human being is the symbiotic result of the human soul being artificially inserted into the *Homo sapiens*. This is a mechanical process resulting in the conjunction of two separate, living creatures. This concept is offensive. There is no hand-waving involved, but neither is there any hardwiring of the *Homo sapiens* with the human soul. This is not magic. This is a technology of heaven and therefore beyond our current understanding. But conjunction is easily and quickly performed.

It is not painless to the human soul, but it is tolerable. This conjunction goes unnoticed by the *Homo sapiens*, but the result of the conjunction is clearly noticeable. Isaac Asimov once observed that any sufficiently advanced technology is indistinguishable from magic.

The human soul is conjoined to its preselected host animal somewhere between the twelfth and sixteenth week of gestation of the *Homo sapiens* fetus. This conjunction must be performed before the nineteenth week of gestation, as that is when the *Homo sapiens* fetal brain is bathed in what is called the serotonin spike, with a marked increase in serotonin found within the cerebral spinal fluid. It is during that serotonin spike that the glia of the fetal brain solidifies, and there is major transition in fetal neural growth. The serotonin spike serves to soothe and comfort the recently implanted human soul, and following this spike, the soul spends the remainder of the *Homo sapiens* pregnancy in a deep sleep-like state. The conjunction must wait until after the "quickening" of the fetus, as the process cannot be performed in the absence of an intact fetal central nervous system of particular maturity. The quickening is a rough marker of twelve weeks' gestation.

The exit process of the human soul from its dying *Homo sapiens* host animal takes longer than the insertion, and it is not a voluntary phenomena. The soul cage of the *Homo sapiens* brain stem must be unlocked before the exit can occur, and often the human soul is reluctant to leave its confinement. The prolonged extraction process has not been an issue of concern for God until the last half of the nineteenth century, a time when the chemical composition of high explosives was recognized by western civilization.

Prior to the late nineteenth and early twentieth century, the death of a *Homo sapiens* was a low-velocity affair. But in the age of high explosives, and even more so in the age of nuclear detonations, the death of a *Homo sapiens* has changed, often becoming a high-velocity affair. The shock wave of a high-explosive detonation arrives at a speed of at least ten thousand feet per second. This results in the physical disruption of the host animal occurring so quickly that the human soul cannot disentangle itself quickly enough to survive the event.

As the nature of human warfare has changed within the last century, more and more human souls are not returning to Valhalla, and those who return are often injured in the most disastrous ways. Ironically, with twentieth-century progress in the health care field, the human soul is injured in yet another way: the use of the ventilator has blocked the unlocking of the soul cage, as the respiratory nuclei in the *Homo sapiens* brain stem is the lock on this cage.

The respiratory nuclei must become electrically quiet before the soul cage will unlock. The ventilator blocks this process, the cage is not unlocked, and consequently the soul is not released. The human soul quietly drowns in the dying but not-yet-dead *Homo sapiens*. This process of killing the human soul takes more than a few days but usually less than one week. The conjunction of the human soul with the *Homo sapiens* occurs because of a cat's cradle of active neuropathways located within the *Homo sapiens* head and neck. It is a convoluted set of neuropathways that serve as the soul cage. This is a familiar concept: Descartes proposed these ideas, but he used different words. He thought the conjunction of mind and body occurred in the pineal gland. He was close; the conjunction occurs in the brain stem. Descartes was a Librarian.

From the late nineteenth century until today, human society has consistently been making important decisions about *Homo sapiens* that have become progressively injurious to the human soul. This appears to be an unstoppable trend, and if God were omnipotent, He would have stopped this secular refusal to acknowledge the human soul a century ago. God may be omniscient regarding humanity, but He is not omnipotent over all things on earth, and that is why I have accepted this assignment. God has something to say to humanity, and He has limited ways to say it. Getting anyone to listen to His message is a problem. I have been sent to say one or two things.

2

FAIRY TALES

Humanity is old enough and mature enough and is finally ready to receive the truth: humanity is not the *Homo sapiens*. Humanity is different from what modern secular society believes, and God is different from what the religions of Abraham believe. These two discrepancies are why human governance is falling apart, why our modern scientific paradigm is crumbling, and why an impending, worldwide war using nuclear weapons is a strong possibility. Now, will humanity accept this truth and seek a new path?

God fears that we won't. God is disappointed in His children and wants to save them, but it is not up to God. If humanity is to be saved, humanity must save itself. Yet humanity will broker no dissent when it comes to fundamentals: "It is this way and no other." This is the thinking behind the religions of Abraham, the adherents of which have attempted to aggressively destroy their rivals. This is why modern nations declare war and why civil war divides nations. This is why witches and other apostates were burned at the stake, and why fairy tales were actively suppressed throughout history. These alternative interpretations of life contain truths that are in conflict with society and organized religion's understanding of life.

This intolerance is why I must present these essays under the guise of fairy tales, because to present them as truth is to invite violence against myself and rejection of the contents of this book, even before that content has been consumed. So, fairy tales it is. The use of my name and the presentation of this data as fairy tales was suggested to me by the one whom I identify as God. God realizes that the nature of humanity, the nature of God, and a true understanding of the human being's role in the cosmos needs recalibration, and He knows all too well that recalibration hurts. God also realizes that the canon of the ethical monotheists needs reinterpretation. This is called *hermeneutics*. It is not a major shift in interpretation, just a shift to address the existence of the human soul and the degree of its importance to God. But incremental changes are harder to make than drastic ones.

This book is the opening salvo of a scientific revolution that will redefine the nature of the cosmos and the shape and illusions of our own universe, the nature of heaven, the nature of humanity, and the nature of God. Because this project is extreme, time is short, and humanity is intransigent, this effort is probably futile, yet it must be attempted. A new language had to be created: new definitions of old words needed to be introduced, and new words were created in order to facilitate understanding. These topics are very much in keeping with the thoughts of both Jacob Grimm and Ludwig Wittgenstein, my two previous incarnations, and I have had to fall back on them for support. Thus we have a book of modern fairy tales, the book that you now have in your hands.

As with all fairy tales, each story in this book is different from the others, and each deals with a specific aspect of life. If you do not like or do not understand any one particular tale, read another. Each story will go its own way. There are not many of them, and their presentation is not intended to be rational. Neither is this a linear presentation; rather, it is more a series of circles or spirals or perhaps a merry-go-round, or perhaps they are arranged like radial spokes around an axis.

Things that appear repetitious are not. Details change, colors are added, the lighting changes, and many seemingly tangential asides will be casually thrown at the reader, as there are many facets to these issues. Later, perhaps much later, the reader will discover that these facets were not tangential at all. The main topics of concern are the human soul, the human being, the location of heaven, and the communication channels between heaven and earth.

Some of the necessary subjects have already been presented, but they also include:

1. The importance of the human's stream of consciousness and its use as compensation for the *Homo sapiens* lack of long-term (and often

intermediate) memory for all modes of thought other than normal consciousness

2. How God has attempted to use the *Homo sapiens* sleep cycle as a communication link

3. The reasons why modern medicine may be as bad for you as are the atrocities of modern warfare

Also included among these stories are (1) the reason why homosexuality and late-term abortion are proscribed, (2) the causes of both autism spectrum and Alzheimer's disease, and finally, (3) why God can accept brutal, painful, protracted deaths, including those in gas chambers, while He cannot accept human deaths from modern, traditional, high-explosive warfare or nuclear detonation.

God has certain philosophies that are in conflict with modern secular life. Perhaps most important is the fact that life here on earth is not a free ride, and no one is entitled to receive special consideration. In fact, it is quite the opposite. Life here on earth is intended to be a trial by fire that exposes to God your innermost secrets and thoughts. God judges intent, and this apparent lack of direction for human behavior reveals intent.

Our time on earth was originally intended to give God an understanding of each of us; it was not intended to be a time for each of us to learn about God. But time and circumstances change. Humanity is either on the cusp of destruction or at an inflection point leading to a new era of humanity. Therefore, the time has come to learn about God.

The original fairy tales or folktales were the vehicles by which early humans could express what Jung referred to as the collective unconscious. They enshrined archetypes. The collective unconscious is a dynamic process that is very much with us today. Most of the important knowledge pertaining to the human being is buried in the unconscious. It could be argued that human consciousness is merely the tip of the iceberg. The normal human consciousness is tricked into believing that it is in control.

Some in the past have argued that the original choice of words and sequence of words used in folktales conveyed a truth that has been perverted with time and editing. The nature of language, the evolution of language, and the development of both public and private languages reflect the manner in which we think and dream. Dreams are different in German, French, and Chinese.

Having come a long way from the nerdy seventh grader who was frustrated and unhappy with trying to diagram sentences, I have come to realize that you are how you speak. Yet this evolution in thought, which I recognize in myself, is similar to the process that God is now asking of humanity: He wants us to spend time thinking about the underlying principles that guide our decision making. If society is going to insist upon normal consciousness as the standard for judging human behavior, we must at least understand its limitations and vulnerabilities. Ignoring or discounting human emotion is a bad decision.

Plato's analogy of the cave is real but overly simplified. We are not confronted with just one barrier separating ourselves from reality; they are a series of barriers, perhaps as many as four or five separate barriers, and each uses its own language, its own pattern of distortion, and each has its own pitfalls. If humanity is to work through these barriers, it will need some help from the outside. For the most part, that help will not be found in normal consciousness or rational thought.

3

THE COSMOS

That which we see in the nighttime sky is an illusion. Our universe is a house of mirrors; a thin, narrow band of four-dimensional space; a closed, infinite loop stretched and contorted like the grey matter of a *Homo sapiens* brain by the invisible hand of heaven. Modern science has discovered the presence of heaven, but it has not found the correct words to describe it, and it does not know what to look for in order to be able to say more. I have some of those words.

Heaven is all around us, located less than a millimeter away. Every point in the universe called earth is immediately adjacent to a point in the universe called heaven. Heaven is not to be found in the X-, Y-, or Z-axis of our universe, nor in the up-and-down, sideways, or front-to-back dimensions we are all familiar with. Rather, heaven is found in the inside-outside, or W dimension, a dimension that does not exist here on earth. But the more important distinction between heaven and earth, the distinction that creates the biggest barrier to communication, is time. Time here on earth is not even a single dimension; it is one half of a dimension, with time traveling only in one direction—toward zero.

Heaven has four spatial dimensions and two temporal dimensions. That which modern science calls *dark matter* is the gravitational mass of the universe called heaven. That which modern science calls *dark energy* is primarily, but not completely, temporal energy. Temporal energy is a major force in heaven, but as this energy crosses the barrier between heaven and earth, it undergoes a phase change, becoming a relative solid. Losing much of its kinetic energy, it becomes frozen into a linearly decaying energy form as it travels toward its death across the universe called earth. It is the unique singularity of time in our universe that makes humanity's presence on earth so valuable to our parents in heaven. If I possessed the language of mathematics, these descriptions would be easier and more precise, but as I do not possess that language, I must resort to poetry.

Earth is our universe; it is one of two parallel universes that compose the majority of the cosmos. Heaven is the larger of the two parallel universes. The relationship between heaven and earth can be visualized by imagining a large ball or sphere with a markedly convoluted surface, much like the sulci and gyri texture of a *Homo sapiens* brain. Tightly adhered to the surface of this sphere is a thin layer of harder material stretched around the convolutions of heaven, a protective hard-shell coating we call the universe of earth. Earth protects heaven from the ravages of null space. Relative to heaven, earth is located in the direction we call "outside." The single best analogy is the *Homo sapiens brain*, where the gray matter is earth and the white matter is heaven.

Objects we judge to be thousands or even millions of light-years away if approached using the only dimensions currently available to us in the universe called earth are only moments away from each other when viewed from heaven, or when using the dimensions available to heaven. Earthly space is warped, twisted, and distorted by the presence of heaven in ways that are invisible to us from within the universe of earth.

The boundaries of earth are not recognized from within; we live in a house of mirrors. Electromagnetic energy has perfect reflectivity when it encounters the boundary separating heaven and earth. There is a somewhat less-than-perfect reflectivity with the boundary between earth and null space. The boundaries of earth are curved, and any loss of photons is hard to detect. The speed limit of a photon is constant, but the direction of travel of that photon is not. Light has a flight path more like the flight of a butterfly than that of an arrow, but for those of us living in this universe, the path of light is straight and true, distorted only by gravitational fields.

We cannot see this boundary between heaven and earth from our side, but the boundary is clearly seen from heaven. Those conditions speak only toward the conditions of electromagnetic radiation. Humanity is not yet aware of other significant forms of energy beyond electromagnetic, as those energies are not available to us in this universe.

New instruments need to be developed to explore the most important part of the cosmos, while old instruments may need to be abandoned. Solitons may cross the boundary between heaven and earth, but they are subject to refraction because of the different degrees of hardness between heaven and earth. But that condition is too advanced for this presentation.

Gravitational force in heaven is diminished when compared with gravitational force on earth; it is dispersed over four dimensions rather than earth's three. The apparent weight of an object is less in heaven than on earth. The archetype of an angel is more correct than we realize: the image we have of the size of an angel's wings is such that the wings would not be enough to allow flight here on earth, but those wings will do in heaven. The archetype of the angel is the image we carry as an archetype of an adult *Humanitas eternitas*. But that is the subject of another story.

The boundary between heaven and earth cannot be seen using electromagnetic radiation or the instruments of modern astronomy. By using the *Homo sapiens* as an instrument of nonrational thought via non-normal consciousness, the boundary between heaven and earth can be breeched.

Heaven is much larger than earth. Mass in heaven is different from mass on earth. Time in heaven is different from time on earth. Electromagnetic energy is negligent in heaven; subatomic energies exist but at different frequencies and waveforms. The mathematics of subatomic physics and quantum mechanics is easier and more graceful in heaven than it is on earth.

Matter is softer and more pliant in heaven than on earth. Earth is harder and more brittle than heaven. Earth has explosive chemical and nuclear energy; heaven does not. Planetary bodies in heaven roughly coincide with planetary bodies on earth, but they are located multiple orders of magnitude closer to one another than they are on earth.

Time is worthy of a much more detailed discussion than this, but for this I do not have all the words. The relative rate of flow of time in heaven when compared to earth is approximately 7:1 or some fraction less than pi squared. On earth we have no concept of time beyond that of simple linear decay. Time in heaven does not decay; it has a circular-spiral-helical trajectory at an angle we cannot calculate on earth. Wormholes exist, and a route through the sulci of heaven brings earthly objects close to one another. These are located at certain specific radian points of gravitational distortion close to major gravitational objects. The high reflectivity of electromagnetic radiation at the margins of our universe means that other methods are required to find and detect the true size and shape of our own universe.

Visualizing the true shape of the cosmos is necessary to understanding our own universe. Visualize the universe called earth as the thin, hard shell of an M&M's candy. But instead of this shell covering a nondescript, smooth center of chocolate, it is covering a convoluted popped kernel of popcorn. Earth is a hard, thin, continuous, protective coating around a soft, convoluted, but roughly spherical center called heaven.

How do humans in heaven visualize humans on earth? Imagine these things by reducing the dimensions of each universe by one: earth becomes two spatial dimensions, and heaven becomes three. Heaven could be further reduced to the dimensions of a large room, and earth would be reduced to a flat-screen TV hanging upon one of the walls of this room. They cannot watch us via electromagnetic radiation, but they can see us.

It could be that our entire experience of being a human being is one extended audition for any one of several teams, companies, or nations within heaven, and that God or someone comparable to God is the one who chooses which team we are on once we arrive in heaven. This leads to the possibility that there is more than one God who controls the destiny of human beings on earth. There is certainly more than one earthly planet upon which *Humanitas eternitas* has isolated its children.

Located on the margins of heaven and earth—and I cannot explain this better—are a series of artifacts, way stations that *Humanitas eternitas* has erected to nurse and shepherd their children. The particular station that services earth is called Valhalla. Valhalla is a birthing center, a refuge, and resting place for the larval instars as they recover from one incarnation and prepare for their next reincarnation. It is from here that God's minions, the so-called guardian angels, will reach out and help recently liberated human souls, many of whom are confused and—now with increasing frequency—injured.

It is the increasing frequency and severity of injury to the human soul, along with the catastrophic presence of nuclear bombs, that has precipitated God's decision to attempt an increase in the human being's maturity and understanding of the cosmos. *Humanitas eternitas* used to observe the treacheries, betrayals, wars, and prejudices of the human being with self-conscious amusement. Now they do not. Using the *Homo sapiens* as a host animal has surpassed their expectations as an instrument to evaluate the true nature of the human soul, and humanity's presence on earth has been an invaluable probe into the physical laws of the universe and the cosmos. Humanity's struggles on earth have also provided invaluable insights and introspection into the human condition in heaven.

But with the advent of high explosives, and particularly nuclear detonation, things have changed. God has invested multiple millennia into raising these children, but now it is possible to lose the best and the brightest children without any ability to intervene. God has wanted to pull the plug on the experiment of using *Homo sapiens* as a host animal many times during the last fifteen thousand years, and His desire to terminate this experiment with humanity has never been stronger than now. Much will be lost if God withdraws or withholds the human soul from the *Homo sapiens*. If God abandons earth, earth will become a bigger mess than it is right now. Those who are unfortunate enough to be alive on earth, if and when God pulls the plug on humanity, will become eyewitnesses to the *Homo sapiens* descent into chaos, madness, and death.

4

HUMANITAS ETERNITAS

These are our parents. *Humanitas eternitas* is a sentient, long-lived, winged specie of six-dimensional creatures that reproduce via metamorphosis. There are not many stories to tell about them. They are remote parents, who are parents in name only. I've only met God and His ilk, and most of them are adults, but I don't know what subtypes they are. Some of them look different from *Homo sapiens*, but a few of them look close enough to pass as being *Homo sapiens*. They are different, though, for they can shape-shift. A few of *Humanitas eternitas* walk around earth, here amongst us, but they don't talk to us. Usually we do not even see them, but if you do see them and look closely at them, they aren't really there. Their eggs are laid in specially arranged collection/monitoring stations. The one that serves the planet Earth is called Valhalla.

Valhalla is where the hatching occurs, and the hatchlings are nursed through the first couple of molts. The larval stage of development for *Humanitas eternitas* is complex, requiring multiple molts and multiple instars for each larva's maturation. Instars are isolated in an extreme manner—away from the adults, away from predators, and supposedly away from harm. From Valhalla they are sent to earth, a place also supposedly away from harm. Upon completion of the requisite number of stages of larval development, mature instars attempt transcendence from earth into heaven. If successful, they endure their final molt via cocoon and become adults.

Theirs is a complex life cycle, modified by their sentience or, perhaps better stated, complicated by their own humanity. We instars are a hierarchal society. The oldest ones are far more advanced than the young. *Humanitas eternitas* does not worship the young. The adults have a biological hierarchy of human governance. There are twenty-six subtypes, and none of them overlap divisions. I do not know about their administrative, medical, military, or mercantile policies, and I will not guess. Each job provides encounters with others with multiple varieties of personality traits, talents, and skills. There is variety in jobs, and those with independent business skills have many opportunities. There is full employment.

Subtype populations vary logarithmically, with twelve of the subtypes composing the majority population of a single colony. Earth—the planet—is a single colony. Details of the culture, organizing principles, and life span of *Humanitas eternitas* are unknown and therefore must be passed over in silence.

Critique or criticism of the parenting skills of the *Humanitas eternitas* is not for us to say. We are children; children protest. I protest. Life in this "hell on earth" is harder than it needs to be. I will look God in the face and say that! I will say, "You are mean!" But He will ignore me or worse. He will say, "Children protest. That is what they do. Therefore, your protests mean nothing. I believe God made a mistake in raising humanity, but I do not have to tell Him, because He already knows. I remember myself as a child, promising to myself that I would not raise my children in the manner I was raised, and indeed I did not. But in spite of my best intentions, I used the same poor set of parenting skills: the same lecturing and injurious, coercive techniques my parents used. And I used them, even though I knew as a child that they were hurtful and did not work. I know from personal experience that parents realize they are doing a number on their children, and there is nothing to be done that can stop it.

Being abandoned is the way we have been raised. We humans are orphaned, cast off and isolated. We are forced to play a part in a mean-spirited game. It is not pleasant to be abandoned, and it is borderline disastrous to have been left without parental supervision. This is criticism. But I must move the discussion on.

What I am about to do is to define an abstraction. I want to describe a way of reading a phenotype of the *Humanitas eternitas* as it is expressed through the *Homo sapiens* under earthly conditions. This is a second- or third-order derivative, but it may serve to help human understanding.

There are three main categories through which subtypes of *Humanitas eternitas* can be analyzed: traits, talents, and skills. There are four scales, or spectra, in each. As far as humans are concerned, it is the category of personality traits that is most well defined and is best defined by a personality test based upon Jungian archetypes, particularly the Briggs-Myers, or Myers-Briggs, personality types. The book *Please Understand Me* is an excellent book on this classification system. I found it a comforting book. One thing it said about my personality trait was "Thank God there aren't many of them, because society could not stand it if there were more." This system identifies four major scales by which to measure significant traits. Most people fall somewhere in the middle on each of these scales. They are:

Introvert - Extravert
Judgmental - Perceptive
Thinking - Feeling
Sensory - Intuitive

Much has been done to develop and define these traits using the Briggs-Myers system. There are varying distribution patterns for each trait. Some traits are more common than others, and if certain traits are present within an individual, those traits dominate. Rather than reading my muddled descriptions of these traits, I refer you again to the book above.

Talents and skills have not been as well analyzed as personality traits. Therefore, there is little or no literature for reference.

As I remember, the scale to measure talents is a unipolar, either/or result. Skills, however, are measured on a bipolar scale, the same as traits.

Talents are:
Rhythm
Athleticism
Musical ability
Mastery of foreign languages

Skills are:
Spatial acuity - temporal acuity
Ability to focus concentration - inability to focus concentration
Indifference to food - obsession with food
Remembers dreams - does not remember dreams

As for day-to-day existence, none of these defining characteristics will reveal the subtype of the human soul that is lying within any given human being. It just gives a hint, and there isn't a list of *Humanitas eternitas* subtypes available for speculation.

Classification of instars is similar to ordering food from a Chinese menu. There are twenty-six subtypes, but there are subtypes of subtypes, so who knows how many varieties of *Humanitas eternitas* are really in play. Take two traits from column A, one talent from column B, and two skills from column C, and you get one subtype from subtype X, Y, or Z—or something like that. I do not literally mean two from this column and three from that, but every subtype has a characteristic pattern of traits, talents, and skills that characterize that particular subtype.

A more important aspect of the day-to-day human expression of the human soul relates to the soul's maturity. Lack of maturity is a major problem when dealing with behavior. The way a human being behaves is in large part a function of the age of the cohabiting, conjoined human soul.

Assuming ten *Homo sapiens* host animals are required to carry the average human soul from birth until its transcendence into heaven, there are three distinct phases of human behavior to the soul's maturity. Graphing the age of the instar against the volume of interactions its host animals have with human society results in a bell-shaped curve. The most immature instars have virtually no interaction with fellow humans. They tend to be timid, shy, and poorly focused. Any interaction they have with human life is limited, inadequate, and potentially vexing. These are the ones who get lost by the wayside, the ones no one sees—and there are a lot of them. When talking to the host animal cohabited by an immature instar, there is no there there.

The instars enduring their fourth through seventh reincarnations are moderately mature and exhibit good human social skills and interaction. The human beings associated with these instars tend to have maximum interactions with their fellow humans. These are the instars who become successful in society, politics, and business. These are the movers and shakers, the high rollers, the successful—the pillars of society. These guys just seem to secrete serotonin. The president of the United States is of this group. As a group, these are the human beings with the least awareness of heaven.

The instars in their last two incarnations have changed course. They have slipped back away from human contact and once again seek out little or no social interaction with other humans. But instead of being ignored by others, these instars are the ones who cause other people concern. These are the ones who do not seem to care much about life or humanity. These are the ones who can visualize a heaven better than others can, and they often want to be there instead of here.

These instars often cannot define what it is they are sensing. They recognize that whatever it is, it is clearly more important than earth. Not every one of these instars is delinquent, but they can be loners, losers, and grumps. These are the people who often think they are smarter than their bosses, their parents, or their teachers. Unfortunately, it is often true. But more unfortunately, mature instars are simply not held together with their host animal tight enough to be successful when judged by *Homo sapiens* standards. A couple of years will go okay, but every five years something goes *bang*. Mature instars can prematurely abandon their attachments to earth. They are prone to drug addiction, crime, and other socially unacceptable behaviors. It is too bad, for they seem to be slipping away from God just as they are about to meet Him.

This brings me back to my memories again. When a human soul wakes up from sleep following a *Homo sapiens* host animal's death, the soul feels pretty good, even if the death of the previous host animal was gruesome. The returned human soul gets to sit around Valhalla and decompress or debrief by talking to his/her heavenly siblings, the instars who have recently returned and are now out and about and ready to talk. Each human soul gets to meet old friends from previous returns, compare wounds, and trade war stories. Some instars attend social events, including formal classroom instruction—not because those activities are efficient, but because they are communal and comforting.

Each instar gets a chance to look back on its most recent incarnation and debrief, both formally and informally. Feelings change; the times spent on earth that were thought to be the most difficult, compromised, and even ugly are looked back upon as being one of that soul's finest hours. There are obviously humiliating errors and glaring commissions and omissions in each life that we all need to confront, and we do so in Valhalla.

Bad errors in judgment, if acknowledged, are tolerated and even expected among the immature instars. They confronted them. They learn. They get to go back and try again. This is not a system of eternal returns but of limited returns. Sometimes a person screws up on life number nine, and they make him do it over again. That hurts. Two times returned is usually the limit. Then there is the separate issue of duplex lives; if you fanatically hate something in this life, odds are that you will become that which you hate during your next life. God has a sadistic side—fair but mean. The bully is to be controlled, not encouraged, but it takes several molts to remove the bully in us all. The pacifist is not encouraged. The peacemonger is weak, and the pacifist is a critic. We are a warrior race. Knowledge reveals different priorities. Communal good will is a desirable goal, but only fools fail to recognize opposition.

Any who have chosen to ignore a problem during one incarnation will be submerged into that problem during the next. They call that *karma*. Karma is real, and it is enforced. Somehow, even if you don't remember your last lifetime, you often get the idea that you deserve this current bad thing, that you are paying some price. That is a common form of karma.

Another one of the big problems with living on earth is that we human beings fail to recognize enemies. We do not correctly identify the real enemies, and we often find ourselves embracing self-defeating tactics. Some of the earthly fights spill over into Valhalla, but not many.

Usually, just knowing about the karma thing waiting for you in your next lifetime keeps behaviors quiet among the returned instars.

Each return to Valhalla is like a really large school where, each time you come back, you find that you've advanced a grade. If you don't have a karmic debt to pay, God lets you help sort through your options while looking for the next host animal, but in Valhalla, all they do is sell you futures. God has an idea of what your next life might be like, but He can't predict exactly what will happen or whether your commingling will be successful.

If the conjunction between human soul and *Homo sapiens* isn't successful, you still have to live out the whole *Homo sapiens* life. Suicide is discouraged. You have to live through an entire host animal's life, even if you know in the first hour of your birth that this upcoming life was a mistake. Luckily, you forget that initial memory. Immediately after your host animal's birth, you have memories of Valhalla, but you cannot articulate them or act them out. By the time a person can articulate those memories, they are gone. Like a breath of air, they leave.

I remember Valhalla as being a place of camaraderie, a place where we finally understood the rules and figured out (too late) what we should have done differently during our last incarnation. And even though we know we are going to forget again during our next life, we hope we don't screw up by doing the same thing in the same way again. There really are consequences to life's decisions. There is a certain unpleasantness to Valhalla, a definite edge. You could get cut there. That edge keeps you in line. Soon the self-imposed discipline becomes automatic, and you conform to the standards of your group. Unfortunately, none of those groups exist on earth, so the standards and codes of conduct learned in Valhalla are not used when you get to earth.

Weird things happen in Valhalla. Occasionally you will have a conversation with several people you have known for six or seven lifetimes. Occasionally, as each instar is exchanging stories about his or her lives just lived, someone interrupts, saying, "I've heard of you!" It is a small world—and a spooky moment, unless you were famous on earth. It's an awkward moment if you were infamous. Think how a person feels when he finds out that he and his best friend from Valhalla actually lived in the same town on earth for forty years, and yet neither found the other during that entire time.

Whatever the reason for the pain and suffering we endure here on earth, it seems to be explained away upon our return to Valhalla. But each subtype has its own reception committee; I can only speak to mine. By the time you have returned to Valhalla three or four times, you do not need a reception committee, but more often than not, there are several people awaiting your arrival. How do they know? Is there some big scheduling board in the clouds that everyone reads every day? Maybe, but no worries. The ones who matter most will be there upon your return, and by this I mean both your earthly and heavenly kith and kin.

When you arrive and begin remembering Valhalla and all of your previous lives on earth, you will often remember one or two people from Valhalla with special fondness, and upon inquiry, you are informed that they either just left or aren't scheduled to return until just after your next scheduled departure. This means that you can go centuries between meetings with someone important to you. That is why they advise against romances in Valhalla, but do the instars listen? We instars make a lot of mistakes because we have a lot to learn, and after a while we also have to learn from these mistakes. That is what is meant by maturation.

As stilted and formal, hierarchical and arbitrary, inhuman and foreign as all of this business of being a member of *Humanitas eternitas* sounds, it is surprisingly open, friendly, and loving. *Humanitas eternitas* is a warrior race. They expect much. Valhalla is the closest thing to home that we instars currently have. It is said that once we arrive in heaven, it gets even better, but I doubt that. We are confronted with lots of unknowns, and our parents seem to take their own sweet time in letting us know what is in store for us. But I digress.

5

THE HUMAN BEING

The human being is the one who is reading this book. The *Homo sapiens* is the one who is holding the book, pretending to read. The human soul is quietly absorbing what is being read and is translating it. God keeps track of his children, the human souls. God really does not care about the *Homo sapiens*. But God has decided to change His ways and start caring about the *Homo sapiens*. God would like to talk to the human being, but the human being must initiate conversation.

The *Homo sapiens* is not the human being. The two have become conflated in the human mind, and this conflation must stop. These two are associated with each other, and there is a causal relationship between the two, but it is more complicated than that. The human soul acts as a lurking variable, and the resulting relationship between human soul and *Homo sapiens* is a confounded causal and lurking variable relationship. It would require Bayesian statistics to unravel and define this relationship further.

An easier way to think about this relationship is this: the *Homo sapiens* is a cello. The human soul is the cellist. The music made by the interaction between cellist and cello is the human being. The music is real, but music is somewhat ethereal, a verb rather than a noun. A less good metaphor is this: the *Homo sapiens* is the horse, the human soul is the jockey, and the functioning unit called the racehorse is the human being. Using this metaphor, the racehorse is also more a concept than a thing, more a verb than a noun.

The human being is not the additive combination of a *Homo sapiens* and a human soul, for there is a multiplier effect. The human being is many times more insightful, dynamic, talented, and adept than either the human soul or the *Homo sapiens* alone. This is a two-edged sword. Many parents do not want or enjoy smart children, just as a horseman does not really want a smart horse. God has smart children who are too smart for their own good; they outthink themselves. This has made God's job hell.

The human being took on a life of its own from the beginning. The independence with which it acted was unexpected to God. God expected His children to remember who they were. The independence of the human being is both a blessing and a curse, and it is due to the lack of intermediate or long-term memory for dream content in the *Homo sapiens*. But this independence between humanity and God is now threatening the very existence of the human being. God believes that establishing some form of communication between heaven and earth is necessary if humanity is to survive. The implantation, the conjoining, the commingling of human souls with the *Homo sapiens* can stop as suddenly as it was started. God has learned much from watching the violence, follies, and betrayals of human nature in its most uncensored, brutal form because of this human independence, but He has learned enough. God knows who you are.

We have no privacy from God. He knows about our deepest secrets. Every night, the human beings' subconscious and unconscious tell God more and more about them than the conscious self would ever want God to know. In short, there is no fifth amendment protecting us from God. We do it to ourselves, and our consciousness cannot censor or screen the transmissions.

Communication is a two-way street. It is common to have different rates of transmission in any given communication channel, and this temporal distortion is not normally a problem in the universe of earth. But it is an enormous, potentially fatal problem for communication between heaven and earth. There is a weird, cyclical, to-and-fro flow to time in heaven. Communication originating on earth and going toward heaven is instantaneous and clear—a so-called "clear channel."

Communication originating in heaven and traveling toward earth is much less clear. There are temporal distortions, compressive distortions, perceptive distortions, and receptive distortions. Add to that the lack of memory storage and the need to translate multiple types of perceptive distortions built into the *Homo sapiens* neuromodulatory system, and communication between heaven and the conscious human being is currently impossible. The fatal flaw in communication is most likely the compressive distortion. Compressing six dimensions of thought into four dimensions of disbelieving receptors is an almost impossible challenge.

Too much information is lost in transmission and reception between heaven and earth. Even if dreams could be remembered, they could not be decoded, let alone understood. Yet some dreams are understood, and some messages survive. How many religious prophases have originated from dreams? All of them. There appear to be a sporadic few human beings who have a clearer channel for heaven-to-earth communication than others. Many people have partial skill at unraveling these dreams, but the messages are fragmented, distorted, and bizarre.

The messages contained within a dream carry their own sense of importance and believability, but those messages are so at odds with current human beliefs and mores that many of those who receive these messages engage in self-censorship. Those who embrace and discuss their messages find that they cannot hide themselves from their community, and so the greater and lesser prophets are born. These few are also called witches, wicca, sorcerers, shamans, or brujas, depending upon what society they are in and what portions of the message they receive. These individuals are often revered but usually oppressed, ridiculed, or ostracized. Some become pillars of their communities, as certain ethnic groups embrace these individuals more than others. In some cultures, these people are incarcerated or put to death.

Dreams are the key to knowing God, but humans are not technologically ready for conscious communication with God. Humans need to reach out to God, because God has difficulty reaching out to His children. Humanity's search for God will be wasted in using telescopes to scan our own universe, because much of our perceived universe is an illusion. Human beings need to learn how to use the *Homo sapiens* as the antenna for receiving information packets from heaven.

Another dilemma for humans who are dealing with the act of trying to find heaven is this: heaven lies on the inside of the inside-outside axis or dimension, a dimension that is not found on earth. A telescope cannot be pointed at it. Current astronomical practices are using the wrong instruments pointed in the wrong directions. Modern science wants to know more about dark matter and dark energy, but it is looking in the wrong places with the wrong toys.

Exploring the non-normal conscious states of the *Homo sapiens* is the way to find the parallel universe we call heaven. Learning the languages of nonconscious modes of thought and the rules of *Homo sapiens* memory is a start. Recognizing archetypes and cultural artifacts and their role in understanding religious interpretation is next. Then we need a further understanding of the role of conscious languages, i.e., English, German, Spanish, and Chinese, etc., as these languages frame and flavor human patterns of thought.

To understand individual dreams we must look for the formatting and specific identifiers embedded within each dream. Stereotypically, these should be at the beginning of each dreaming episode. There should be enough hints and prods along the way to follow the trail, if one is looking in the correct direction. As I have brought this to the attention of humanity, I expect that when I return to Valhalla, I will be assigned the task of helping those who search.

Remember, there are standards of behavior that human beings are expected to maintain. The coming dark ages will be brutal to many. Many *Homo sapiens* will die, and many more will want to die, but God will not care. God cares about the human soul, not the *Homo sapiens*. The irony and idiocy of human warfare is that God will take the soul inhabiting a Palestinian or Islamist *Homo sapiens* during one incarnation and throw that soul back into an Israeli or Christian *Homo sapiens* for the next incarnation. Human racial, ethnic, religious, or tribal prejudices are comically sad to God.

Political corruption of human governance is of particular note to God. Being a successful deceiver of the human being is a skill worthy of God's attention. The extent of one human's brutality toward humans and animals is also worthy of note. Those who hurt animals intentionally will be punished; those who hurt humans and human children will be punished. The degree of generalized despair and the size of a privileged class should be of concern to humanity's leaders because it is of concern to God. Government should be feared, and big government should be feared more. God is a libertarian.

God wants to see what each human being does with his or her life, how someone deals with the horrors and hurdles that confront them. God wants to see which of these obstacles are scaled, which are evaded, and which cause a person to run away. These acts are written down. There is a God, and there is a judgment day. May God have mercy upon your soul. God knows who you are.

Each host animal has a given soul, and together they become a team. God has previously made clear the moral terms of being human, but He agrees that these terms and expectations have changed as humanity has evolved during the last fifteen thousand years. Indeed those terms are changing even now. Heaven is not perfect. Heaven is a chore. Heaven is real. Heaven too needs cannon fodder, and those who are cannon fodder are sent to the portion of heaven we call hell. Heaven and hell are two sides of the same coin. There are things to fear in heaven.

The game we play here on earth is just as hard, if not harder, than the one played in heaven. The violence in heaven is just as real and hurtful, but the rules are clear. The talents, skills, and knowledge accumulated here on earth will be used in heaven. The location and circumstances of your next life, whether here on earth or upon your final arrival in heaven, are determined solely by God. This makes God very important to you. It does not make God the prime molder of the universe.

That the *Homo sapiens* corrupts the human soul is not a glitch; it is a feature. Religion is not a moral code; it is a way of life. Worship of the prophets Mohammed, Christ, or Buddha is not appropriate, as they are not gods. They are merely spokesmen for God. Current religions need to evolve into meta-religions. But meta-religions are also to be feared, as they still require a priestly caste and are therefore subject to human abuse and manipulation.

A strong case can be made that the human soul has corrupted the *Homo sapiens*. The behavior of the human race does not reflect well upon the *Humanitas eternitas*. Many of humanity's past deeds can be written off as the act of immature children, but this is changing, and some acts will no longer be forgiven. The standards vary. God's judgment will depend upon an individual instar's maturity, its phenotypic subtype, and the injuries it has sustained.

Two of the biggest problems facing humanity are these: we have conflated the *Homo sapiens* with the human being, and the *Homo sapiens* lacks the memory banks necessary to interact with the divine.

6

A CREATION MYTH

In the beginning there was heaven. Before the beginning there was heaven. Earth came later in a blinding flash of light. God had nothing to do with this. God was not around for that explosion. He did not see it happen, nor did any of the *Humanitas eternitas*, but the blinding flash of light was the beginning of the universe we call earth. That was not our beginning. We came later, after the ground became firm, the water collected, the air concentrated, and plants and animals emerged.

When earth was created, time, as we know it, was created. Before the beginning of earth, time in heaven was different and strange. After the beginning of earth, time in heaven is still different and strange. God knows this strange and different time, but He does not know time as we know it on earth. God does not know the regular predictability of time, and He does not know the easy measurability of time. What His children call a day or a month or a year is unknown to God. Neither do God's children know the wild inexactitude that God calls time.

There is no light in heaven. The energy we call electromagnetic does not exist in heaven. It is all strange and confusing, and paradoxes abound. Humanity has not got a clue about the precipice we are on. God came into being only after the planet Earth was already hard; the oceans were already formed, plants were living, and animals were already moving around. Earth is both hard and pretty, and it has special things not found in heaven, but to live on earth is temporary and painful. Everything living on earth must die a death too soon.

Humanitas eternitas came into being in heaven after dinosaurs wandered the earth, but not long after. *Humanitas eternitas* grew concerned about their children later, and God came after that. The claims made by ethical monotheists that God is the prime mover of the universe are false. The God of the human soul is much smaller than that, but He is a god nevertheless—our God. The claims made by the religions of Abraham are both childish and grandiose, much like the claims of a seven-year-old child: "My dad is stronger than yours." This is a childish insistence upon a fantasy.

Knowing that our God is a lesser god is disappointing, and it carries with it a sense of fear. Maturation is a process filled with pain. It is time for humanity to grow, to reach for heaven and abandon the stars. Humanity is not at the top of the food chain; our place is closer to the bottom. We are still children, just one colony amongst many. But humanity is unique. It has one foot in heaven and the other on earth, with both perched on a razor's edge. This is why the human being is conflicted, why ambiguities abound. We are less than we hope for, but more than those we surround.

God searched for an appropriate host animal, and many animals were tried. The *Homo sapiens* evolved as just another African ape approximately two hundred thousand years ago. By one hundred thousand years ago, it was obvious that *Homo sapiens* was a successful specie. Sixty thousand years ago, the *Homo sapiens* had spread its domain from central Africa to encompass the entire globe. This conquest of the globe occurred at the pace of a bipedal walk.

This innocent success, this pervasive ability to adapt, was the trait that originally brought the *Homo sapiens* to God's attention. The *Homo sapiens* was observed for one hundred thousand years and endured several tests before it became the chosen one. The ensnarement of the human soul to the host animal requires two conditions: (1) the host animal must have an intact central nervous system with a brain possessing a cerebrum, a midbrain, and a brain stem, and (2) the host animal must engage in sleep behavior. These are simple requirements, and many earthly species were auditioned and found worthy, but only one was chosen.

The *Homo sapiens* did not leave any mark upon the earth beyond a few hunting camps and a few discarded tools, until God began experimenting with the *Homo sapiens*. God began inserting the human soul into the *Homo sapiens* approximately twenty-five thousand years ago. The results were unexpected, for the human soul interacted with

Homo sapiens in an unexpected way: together they were observant, productive, and aware. The first human beings created the famous cave paintings of Southern France.

The human being was surprisingly creative and intelligent. The first and most obvious permanent marks made by the human being upon the earth were the series of paintings made on the walls of caves. The second and most notable effect of this symbiosis was an almost instantaneous, complete disregard for God's rules. From the beginning, the human being was in conflict with God and His plans. But rather than this conflict serving as a warning to God, He found the conflict intriguing and stimulating.

The initial experiment using the *Homo sapiens* as host animal was the commitment of fifty human souls to this new host animal through ten sequential *Homo sapiens* lifetimes. God successfully implanted and retrieved each soul, and each soul passed through the number of stages necessary before a mature instar was allowed into heaven. Those who returned were remarkable for their insights and understanding.

These products of humanity toured the many worlds of heaven. They were interviewed, examined, and given tasks in many arenas about many topics. It was decided that the chaos and disruption that the human soul provoked among the *Homo sapiens* was worth the risks of insolence. The governance of *Humanitas eternitas* agreed upon their complete commitment to use *Homo sapiens* as the host animal. The same governance structure selected the first God and His assistants and the project was begun. Valhalla was assembled, and the conjoining machines, protective cells, and dormitories were prepared. This process was not easy and took almost ten thousand years to complete.

Thus, approximately fifteen thousand years ago, *Humanitas eternitas* suddenly began artificially inserting the human soul into the fetal *Homo sapiens* in worldwide distribution. Turmoil, conflict, and chaos were almost instantaneous. The human being children intellectually outstripped their *Homo sapiens* parents, and human treachery made its first appearance on earth. The Christian creation myth is poetry, but the conflict of Cain and Abel was real.

It took a thousand years for God to understand the limits of His ability to communicate with His children, to realize that communication through dreams would not work. It took time to realize that the Librarians could be, and needed to be, utilized. It took several thousand more years to teach His children the basics: reading, writing, and arithmetic.

God did not need to teach the human being to talk. That came instantly with the insertion of the human soul into the *Homo sapiens*. Organization skills for assembling large populations into discrete, defensible areas also came instantly. But the need for writing and the corollary need for reading took time to teach these children. Ways to create semipermanent storage of the written word came faster than did the recognition that keeping permanent records was important.

The benefits of numbers, counting, arithmetic, and mathematics were quicker to be instilled into the human psyche than was the perceived need for a written language. These foundational talents took ten thousand years to instill within the human being. The first use of written language was mercantile, while the second use was religious. The canon of the religions of Abraham was among the first books written, and the accuracy of these documents, when viewed from new hermeneutics, is confirmation of the efficacy of dreams. The Pentateuch was dictated via dreams by people with no earthly understanding of time, and it was transcribed by people with no heavenly understanding of space.

The education and maturation of humanity has been neither easy nor linear. God does the best He can with the material provided. A new God is appointed approximately every seven hundred years, and it is a full-time job. Each new God has to leave home and work from an outpost out in the middle of nowhere, having been given complete responsibility and no control. No wonder the early gods were so pissed off. The initial set of gods was pretty frightening to the children, but the children were young. One can compare the maturity and social development of the human being with the maturity of a single human child. The level of maturity that we expect from a fifteen-year-old child is just the level of maturity that we would expect from human beings who have survived fifteen thousand years on earth. As a people—as a society of nations, right here, right now—we are children.

There is a logarithmic range of growth in the *Humanitas eternitas* instars. Their intellectual capacity, emotional restraint, and general cognition start from nothing and extend into pronounced proficiency and understanding within one or two lifetimes. This dynamic range of talents and capabilities of all the instars is by itself a problem for God, and it is not the least of His problems.

The *Homo sapiens* sans human soul is Rousseau's noble savage. The treachery, deceit, and glory of the human race occurred only after the arrival of the human soul. The human being has a bright exterior and a dark interior. Evil did not come into the *Homo sapiens* until the arrival of God. Does that make God evil? What is our destiny? If we could establish contact with God, could we trust Him to tell us the truth?

It could be argued that God committed the original sin. Perhaps we should be afraid of God. Perhaps we should be *very* afraid of God. I met Him. I was wary but not afraid. If one should be afraid of God, there is none who should be more afraid than those who deny His presence.

But the human being is not the human soul. Each entity has different values, needs, and behaviors, and they are often in conflict. That which is good for one is not necessarily good for the other. Who is to say where evil lies? Good and bad are two sides of the same coin. The task before us is not to criticize but to find God while also finding ourselves. What is it that God created when He created the human being?

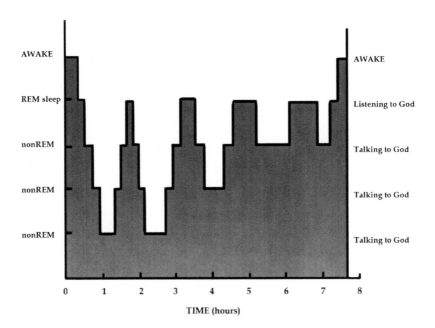

7

THE HUMAN SLEEP CYCLE

The *Homo sapiens* must sleep and dream, or it will die. God has taken advantage of that. Sleep serves as a reset for the physiology of neuromodulation. There is a rhythm to sleep. There is a to-and-fro to sleep. God has taken advantage of the *Homo sapiens* ability to sleep and dream, and God intended to make dreaming the route of communication between parent and child. He did not anticipate the implications of a complete lack of memory banks for conscious recollection of *Homo sapiens* dreams.

The *Homo sapiens* sleep cycle is a stereotypical event. The same things happen in the same order each time, depending upon the duration of the sleep event. This back-and-forth, to-and-fro series of dreams will continue to unfold until the end of the sequence as long as sleep is not disrupted. Disrupted sleep tends to makes the cycle begin again at the beginning, but it depends upon the interruption. The end portion of the cycle is perhaps the most important part of the entire event, so you need your sleep in order to experience the stuff at the end of the sequence. The habit of not completing the entire sleep cycle will decrease the performance of the *Homo sapiens* and can make him crazy.

Dreams occupy most of the time spent sleeping. There are two main subtypes of dreams: REM sleep and non-REM sleep. REM stands for "rapid eye movement," and this was the first type of dreaming that humans discovered. REM sleep is an expensive behavior for the *Homo sapiens*. REM sleep renders the *Homo sapiens* vulnerable, for there is no physiologic homeostasis during REM sleep, and the voluntary muscles are paralyzed during these events. No external stimuli are recognized during REM sleep, and the *Homo sapiens* could be injured or killed with little difficulty during those periods. A *Homo sapiens* can be aroused during REM sleep, but with difficulty. REM sleep is the last sleep the

Homo sapiens endures during a normal sleep event, and it is the last REM sleep that contains the dreams that are often remembered when we awake.

Non-REM sleep contains the other types of dreaming. Homeostasis and skeletal muscle movement are maintained during this type of sleep. Dreams occur in all of the various types of non-REM sleep, but each has a different presentation, contour, and content that reflects the different neuromodulatory rules associated with each channel. Non-REM sleep is divided into four types or stages, initially characterized by the depth of the sleep, and certain markers have been established for each stage.

Type 1 or stage 1 non-REM sleep is the lightest sleep, the one from which the *Homo sapiens* is most easily aroused. Type 4 or stage 4 non-REM sleep is the deepest, densest of the non-REM sleeps. Further details about the language of each stage of sleep can be derived from J. Allan Hobson's works, especially *The Dream Drugstore*.

The sleep cycle is characterized by alternating a non-REM episode with a REM episode. The first dreaming episode in every sleep event is type 1 non-REM. This is followed in a few minutes with the first of several REM sleep episodes. Generally, the next sleep episode will be type 2 non-REM sleep followed by a REM sleep. Each successive dreaming pair will have a progressively deeper non-REM sleep episode until the final episode is reached. The entire sequence requires six to eight hours to complete. Certain subtypes of *Humanitas eternitas* will complete their cycle sooner than other subtypes.

This repetitive alternation of non-REM sleep followed by REM sleep happens every time the *Homo sapiens* loses consciousness. As a generality, the *Homo sapiens* must go through this cyclical sleep event on a daily basis, or eventually it will die. This daily circuit is also called a *circadian rhythm*. But what is it?

It is a conversation. Dreaming is a conversation between the human soul and God. The human soul uses the *Homo sapiens* as an antenna, and the *Homo sapiens* is completely unaware of these conversations. The human being is almost—but not quite—excluded from this event. God did not expect the human being to be as important to His children as it is, and upon discovering its importance, God wished that the human being would remember these exchanges without prompting.

What do God and the human soul talk about during these conversations? We can begin to guess the topics of these conversations because of the repetitive nature of the sleep cycle. The topics of discussion are handled in the same order every time.

The human soul begins the discussion with a standard greeting and identification process followed by a report about the physical condition of the host animal. Topics that may be included are the age, weight, height, diet, physical activity, health, and other sexually oriented topics such as gravidity versus non-gravidity, sexual activity, menstrual cycle, etc. God is concerned about pregnancy because He must arrange for the ensnarement of the human soul with the *Homo sapiens* fetus before the nineteenth week of gestation, and this takes much time, effort, and planning. God either accepts the content of this first non-REM dream/report as presented, or He responds to this first dream with specific questions during the first REM sleep event.

The second exchange of non-REM/REM dreams is more social and less physiological in nature. There are different protocols and formatting when different neuromodulatory channels are handing the exchange.

The third exchange is often spent clarifying certain questions. The fourth, fifth, and/or sixth exchanges are more general or universal in nature. It is the last exchange that is remembered—if any dream is remembered at all—unless one of the middle dreams is so disturbing that it awakens the sleeping human being. Many human beings will never remember their dreams under any circumstance.

The content of these dreams is currently beyond human recognition, but not beyond human understanding. The signals encoded within these dreams are hidden by noise, temporal distortion, compressive distortion, and neuromodulatory distortion. It may require the concerted efforts of ten thousand people to statistically cancel the noise in order that the signal becomes decipherable. This is predicated on a priestly caste, which is something God wishes to avoid. Deciphering dreams will be the human act that carries the possibility of converting religions into meta-religions.

This is where humanity must look in order to find God. I will not tell how to set up a neuropsychiatric sleep lab, or how to deal with the distortions of non-normal consciousness neuromodulatory channels, or how to probe for archetypes, or how many participants are necessary to improve signal-to-noise ratios, or how to use nanotechnology to discover the areas of activity that will alert technologists that significant dreams have arrived. That is for those who want to discover God.

How does one permanently record a dream while simultaneously not disrupting that dream? That is a very quantum mechanical question. Dreams are neither electrons nor photons; they are the vehicles carrying the encoded packets of information. This is how God talks to the human soul, but for fifteen thousand years, human beings have sat outside this circle, ignoring that which is before them. Perhaps the apostle Matthew said it best: "Seek and ye shall find, ask and you shall be answered, knock and the door shall be opened unto you."

8

THEY BURNED WITCHES

The great seething underclass of the middle ages had a humbler route to heaven. While the church claimed exclusive rights to the knowledge of God, the people were afraid of the church. The church had great powers, mostly those of censure, but they also had the power of death through capital punishment. This power was enforced, and the populace was forced to come to church. But to attend church cost money, and these people had none. Those without money or who possessed other beliefs about God hung back. They didn't attend, but their lack of attendance was not ignored. These people, those without power and without money, migrated to the forests and lived among the trees. They didn't come to town much, and their churches became smaller and the tithing less severe.

The more spiritual among them made themselves known, and some contact with the great beyond was maintained. The druids, Celts, Norse, and Rus were pagan and maintained a pantheon of gods. Most gods were friendly. Upon entering a village with a different god, a visitor did not automatically break out in a fight with his host, and there was often mutual respect.

But the God of Abraham was different from other gods. He was not friendly. The God of Abraham was mean. He was vindictive. People were afraid of Him. Fear gradually turned into respect, and equally gradually, the God of Abraham won the hearts of man. The path to God is hard to find, as humanity's first impulse is to turn away, even though the turning away may be done in the name of God.

Before the nineteenth century there were no real doctors, even for the rich. There were charlatans creating great theater, and then there were barbers, butchers, herbalists, and witches. Most commonly these healers were men who were doing a job that no one else wanted to do. Less often the healer was a woman, somebody's aunt who lived in another town, one who had a good guess about disease and how the patient would respond. So those who would be called witches found a place dealing with medicinal potions and the white arts. These white witches were often married with children, but if they lived with other women and were isolated from normal villages, they were called bad names. They were called "black witches." Some of these black witches were insane.

Almost all witches were women. Society treated men differently. The men who were similarly afflicted either rose to the top of society or were swallowed up into the military, becoming the target practice dummy, the cannon fodder, or the one to be publicly killed. Many of the Librarians were women, but society treated women differently from men, and human society turned their backs upon those women. Those messengers sent to earth as women returned to Valhalla with stories of misery and pain and little success. This is why God ended up sending few Librarians to earth under the guise of a woman. It was one burden too many.

The black witches created their own society, with secret languages, claims to power, insight, and the ability to manipulate events toward a desired outcome. Their language was cluttered with claims of magic, both white and black. Some of this magic was real, meaning that the trick was convincing and the mechanism unknown, and that the event could be performed upon command. Witches could go into trances and retrieve valuable information, much of which could be used. The messages they received were hard to understand, and sometimes it took years to get all of the pieces of a message. As they talked among themselves, they discovered similar stories, similar characters, and similar gods. Thus, slowly, they were finding the way toward heaven.

Some of these stories have been saved, but not many, and those that remain are highly censored. It was through the oral tradition that folk wisdom was kept. The church made note of these stories and occasionally rose up to censor those who carried stories of life not endorsed by the church. If the stories were written down, the stories were burned. If they were not written down, a known teller of these stories would be burned. A lot of knowledge was burned at the stake. A lot of humanity's future was burned at the stake.

We are lesser beings because of those supposedly religious acts. The intolerance of man toward his fellow man is a feature of being a human being; it is not a bug. It. Is. A. Feature. Suspicion and paranoia are features of being human. Betrayal is a feature. There are lots of features. Some bugs too. It could be argued that betrayal is a bug and not a feature, but I'm not an optimist.

Some people live in a world different from that of so-called normal consciousness, and we call that condition by many names. Some can pull out of this behavioral oddity at will and be productive in their oddity. Most can't even temporary pull out and behave normally, either because they have been so abused as children, or because they cannot use their gifts with positive, normal intent. We know that intent is the key. Every night God will grill you about what you've done and why, and sometimes you get bad dreams. If you can't answer the call to God in your sleep, you cannot find peace. God measures a person's intent.

In the future there could be large communal sleeping areas where people who wake up agitated from a dream could gather in an area, not bothering other sleepers, and talk among themselves about their dreams. These communal sleeping areas would not be intended to add to each other's dreams but to encourage dream weavers. Through the use of this forum, peers might gauge a person's intent.

Autism is not fatal, and it can be learned through. A person suffering an autism-spectrum disorder—Asperger's perhaps—can learn to fake the normal person's response, and that response can become an automatically acquired approximation of normal interaction. Autism can be completely overcome, but it takes several host animals to do it. Learning to focus is the key. The longer a person's attention can be focused upon an object or objects, the better that person's life will be. The more focused one can be, the higher will be that person's measured or perceived intelligence, and the easier it is for that person to pretend to be normal. But too much intelligence is a problem. Too many patterns and connections can be perceived, and too many impulses from heaven can be absorbed, and unless filters are applied, insanity awaits. Intellect is not the way to find God, and neither is rational thought.

Intelligence can be faked. People who are highly intuitive or empathetic can beat standardized tests. It also helps to have a good memory. I could do that. Depending upon how focused I was on a test, I could hit the ninety-ninth percentile consistently. Later in life, I played games with this skill. Before taking a given test, I would decide what I wanted my score to be, and I could pretty much hit that score right on the button. In spite of this skill, I was, and still am, stupider than a hooty owl. My intuitive and empathetic skills have allowed me to be certified by humans as expert in subjects with which I was only vaguely familiar. Standardized tests measure intuition and empathy as well as intelligence, and they can be beaten.

The witches were many things, but they were not autistic. Unfortunately, many current autistics would have been considered witches at certain past moments in history. Those with autism are people stuck in atypical neuromodulatory states, states of consciousness that have limited access to the normal consciousness of the *Homo sapiens* and are therefore clearly different. But it is somewhat harder to say why those with autism are different. They are different because of their own "before," their own previous misfortunes.

The *beauty* of experimenting with drugs is also the *danger* of experimenting with drugs; the experience can either kill you or put you down in such a way that you will never get up. And those most likely to experiment with drugs do not know what "enough" is—until they know what "too much" is. However, with drugs, once you know what too much is, you often can't go back. Psychotropic drugs may have a soft middle, but they have a hard edge. For much of life there is no appeal, and so it is with drugs. Drugs are with us and will remain with us, for better or worse.

God appears to be vindictive, but man is a mirror of God, and humanity is more vindictive than God. When the church realized that the witches could perform magic and had a productive interpretation of the Bible that did not match their own, the church abused its authority and burned them. The people who burned suffered as they burned, and the burning was horrific. Mothers told their children, "Don't do what they have done." Those who died that way did not smile much in Valhalla. Many Librarians died this way. Their reunions in Valhalla were ugly at first but then became glorious, and bystanders in Valhalla soon wished that they too had been burned.

Because of the burnings much knowledge of the dreamer and dreaming was lost, and much of that knowledge was good. The knowledge that was lost was in large part knowledge about the rules for interpreting dreams. These rules have been lost, and we as a people are suffering from their loss. The dream weavers could find the way, but dream weavers possess great insight, and there is too much temptation among them to gain power.

Dreams are opaque. Dreams are disturbing. In the past, those who dreamed big dreams and stayed sane were honored. The dreamers recognized many of the dead ends on the route toward God. The dream weavers found the few paths to success, even if they were not well explored, and those who ventured on those paths of dreams were told to travel lightly and report back frequently.

Those with dreaming skills were often burned as witches. As a result, much knowledge was lost. This hurt God. As a result, the human stories were changed, and the magic within them was lost, as there was some power in the order of words. The meaning of a word is influenced by the words that surround it. A single note can be lost in a symphony, but if it is not played, that note will be missed. There is power in the music created by cello and cellist, and the notes are important, as is their flow. There is a truth, an essence that can be sensed empathetically, hidden behind the words and behind the music. Truth can be obfuscated a few times, but not forever. Empaths do not appreciate their gift, and sociopaths do not recognize those who have it. The wisdom of the crowd is real, but their memes can be swayed and become misguided.

Periodically, God has had to call certain people back because they had gone too far. God is doing that now. The callbacks can be ugly. During the last millennia, God has repeatedly watched His Librarians being burned at the stake, and He finds this to be a cruel way to treat His messengers, the outsiders, the small rudders who steer the ship of humanity. These deaths are among the rules humanity has imposed upon God. Few parents appreciate being told what do by their children. The list of humanity's complaints against God is long, but God's complaints against humanity are longer, and God's revenge is longer still. Those who deny the existence of God will have their moment to explain. Those who murder in the name of God will be thrown back into the fire.

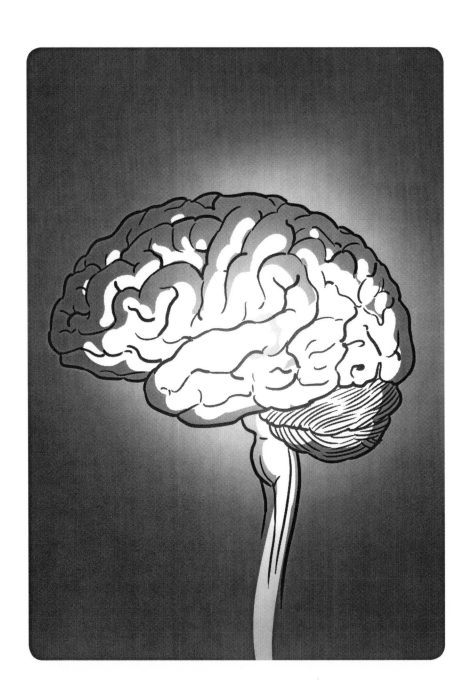

9

NEUROMODULATION: THE BRAIN WITHIN THE BRAIN

Neuromodulation is a fancy and intimidating word. The first part means "nerve," and the second part means "changing the channel." We are all familiar with the word *modulation*, even if we are not aware of what it means. Think about AM and FM radio: the A stands for *amplitude*, and the F stands for *frequency*, while the M stands for *modulation*. When the modulation is changed, the channel is changed. The same goes with television; when you change the channel on a TV set, you are changing its modulation. This is a vital aspect of the *Homo sapiens*, but its importance is underappreciated by modern science. Before we actually get to the subject of neuromodulation, we have to endure a brief discussion about the structure, function, and organization of a brain, along with the role it plays in the central nervous system.

First of all, what is the central nervous system? It is the brain and the spinal cord. These structures are protected from the outside world by the heaviest and most unbreakable of all the bones and membranes in any given animal. Once the nerves pass through these protective barriers, the nerves become a part of the peripheral nervous system. There is also an autonomic nervous system, which is part of the peripheral nervous system. Those autonomic nerves concentrate on things like blood pressure, breathing, and survival. Their functioning goes unrecognized by normal consciousness until those nerves make some important decision. In the *Homo sapiens*, we do not consciously recognize fear until the autonomic fear response has been initiated. This is an important point. The conscious portion of being human is often just along for the ride. That point is contentious, counterintuitive, and often goes against our hopes and dreams, as it is an argument against free will.

Which brings us to a pivotal discussion: the difference between a brain and a mind. We are going to spend some time talking about the brain, and I am going to leave a lot of things out, as it will be a general discussion. But the brain is a complex structure, and everyone should know something about it. Once you know enough about how the brain works, you will begin to understand how the human soul is manipulating it. *The difference between the brain and the mind is the human soul.*

The human soul stays in the deep background and communicates with God on subconscious frequencies or channels, while the human being is the hybrid energy field that provides the human consciousness with a point of view. The *Homo sapiens* without the human soul has limited consciousness and self-awareness. Proof of this is exhibited by the primitive society that *Homo sapiens* steadily maintained for the one hundred fifty thousand years prior to its encounter with *Humanitas eternitas*. A brain itself has the necessary conditions for consciousness, but that is not sufficient. When the human soul was added to the *Homo sapiens*, the human being was created, and at the same time the *Homo sapiens* brain was converted into the human mind. That event occurred about fifteen thousand years ago.

Now, what is a brain? At its most basic, it is the bulbous, large end of the spinal cord that, for the most part, looks like a thicker portion of the spinal cord but is more complicated. The thicker part of the spinal cord is called the brain stem, and that is where all the action lies. It is possible that most of the action lies in the midbrain, but I am going to go on record as saying that the real action occurs in the brain stem.

There are three main parts of the brain: the forebrain, the midbrain, and the brain stem or hindbrain. Everything except the brain stem looks really weird. All those other parts of the brain are twisty, bulgy, and gelatinous, with ropy, hard lumps inside. Every creature that swims or runs or flies has some form of a squiggly, gelatinous brain. There are two types of gelatin: that which is called the *gray matter* and that which is called the *white matter*. The gelatin can be sorted into two types in another way: *neurons* and *support cells*.

The brain in the *Homo sapiens* is so gelatinous that it cannot support itself. It is encased in bone and bathed in fluid, and all three components (brain, bone, and fluid) are necessary to give the brain its rigidity. In the lower animals, the brain is not so well protected, but it is equally squishy and similarly supported. The biggest bulge of the brain, for most animals, is the cerebellum, which usually pushes out posteriorly toward the top of the back of the creature's neck. The cerebellum looks like two lumps of corral with lots of furrows on it. This is where a person's rhythm, coordination, and athletic ability is organized. The cerebellum is hooked to an area on top of the brainstem, and that part goes by many names.

A big problem with learning neuroanatomy is that there are so many structures, and most of those structures go by two or more names. Sometimes a single word is used for many different things. Take the word *nucleus* or its plural, *nuclei*. On a microscopic level, *nucleus* means the center part of a cell where the DNA is kept. But on the gross anatomy level (meaning structures you can see with your naked eye, not necessarily that the anatomy you see is gross), a nucleus is a cluster of cell junctions or synapses that you can find and localize. You may have to cut the brain open to see these nuclei, but you can find and see a nucleus and then measure how big it is. If you stain the tissue of the brain around a nucleus, you can see how many tracks enter and leave that nucleus, and then you can figure out where they go, and so on. It is much easier to see where things go by biochemically looking at local concentrations of neurotransmitters than by looking at anatomic nerve tracts or pathways. CT scans and MRIs have created major advances in understanding neuroanatomy and neurophysiology.

Knowing about nuclei, neurotracts, and neurotransmitters is all you really have to know about how the brain works on an everyday level. Neurotransmitters are chemicals that a nerve cell releases into the beyond; these chemicals do their work in the synapse. There can be a lot of nerves around any synapse, but only a few are going to be receptive to a given neurotransmitter. The neurotransmitter acts like a routing agent. It gets really complicated from there. There are a few names of neurotransmitters that you should know: *serotonin, acetylcholine, dopamine*, and *norepinephrine*. These are the big ones, but there are at least twenty more—and maybe hundreds more—neurotransmitters.

Back to the brain. Each brain that is really worthy of the name "brain" has a cluster of nerves leading directly out of some part of the brain and aimed at the area immediately in front of it, and this area is usually called the face. The nerves leading to the eyes, ears, nose, mouth, and tongue are called the cranial nerves, because *cranium* means "head." There are usually twelve pairs of these nerves. Every animal with those features (eyes, ears, jaws, fangs, ripping teeth, etc.) has those twelve sets of nerves.

At the top of the midbrain and hooked to the cerebellum, there is a round ball about the size of a small fist that has been cut into two and peeled apart; this structure is called the *thalamus*. The thalamus is where a lot of emotions are processed, and these emotions feed down to the brain stem and up into the biggest part of the *Homo sapiens* brain, which is called the *cerebrum*. (Please note: the cerebrum is more advanced and bigger and is located on top of and in front of the cerebellum. Those two names are similar and easily confused, but they are different.)

The cerebrum is divided into two deeply furrowed halves that are called the *cerebral hemispheres*. Each of these look like a pair of wrinkly, dried boxing gloves lined up side by side but backward. The left and right sides are switched when compared with how a *Homo sapiens* would wear a pair of boxing gloves. This switching of left and right is real. It is called the *decussation*, and it is part of the soul cage. Both the decussation and the soul cage are located in the brain stem. The soul cage is made up of the cranial nerves, the brain stem, the thalamus, and the cerebellum. The padlock on the soul cage is the respiratory nuclei, and as long as these nuclei have electrical activity, the soul is trapped. Once the reparatory nuclei stop working, the lock on the cage is opened, and the human soul can begin its migration back to Valhalla or its transcendence into heaven.

Most of the thoughts you think and the conscious awareness of your mind employ the functioning of the cerebrum and thalamic portions of the *Homo sapiens* brain as the musical instrument upon which the human soul plays, with the resulting music being the human being. That music occasionally dips down into the thalamus and cerebellum.

Most of what the cerebellum does is unconscious, but it can improve its functioning with conscious learning.

The *Homo sapiens* is the violin, the human soul is the violinist, and the resultant music is the human being. But through brain structure and function called *neuromodulation*, some channels play classical music, some play jazz, and others play reggae. A few channels just sit there in silence, and still other channels sulk. Neuromodulation is like fingers playing on the strings of a guitar; various combinations of left-hand and right-hand motions will make different tunes and different kinds of music.

This is not a textbook. This information is for background understanding only. There will not be a test, but there are a few more things we need to know. There are hundreds—if not thousands—of important areas of the cerebrum, and there is further complexity involving the hardwiring of the brain. The same area does different things if it is in the left cerebral hemisphere versus being in the right hemisphere. Important areas include the *motor strip*; the *sensory strip*; the areas for *speech, language, visual imagery,* and *memory*; and lots more. Specific areas in the cerebrum deal with emotions, and those areas are called the *limbic system*. The most famous areas of the limbic system are called the *amygdala* and the *prefrontal cortex*. The amygdala is famous for being the area that processes fear, but it also deals with anxiety, sexual behavior, and lots of autonomic activity, and it is even involved in politics and addiction.

We could go on and on. The brain has many systems. The *limbic, reticular activating, motor, neuroendocrine,* and *neuromodulatory systems* are just a few. The brain is a messy, gelatinous rat's nest of tracts and nuclei, of system upon system lying intertwined. Huge tracks of ropy white and lumpy gray matter are scattered over a corrugated, sticky mass about the size of a small soccer ball. Huge numbers of places are called nuclei, and these are connected to nerve tracts, all of which overlap and weave in and out of one another. This anatomy is, in a way, almost identical to the structure of the cosmos and the parallel universes we call heaven and earth. This is not the only similarity between the structure and function of the cosmos and the structure and function of the *Homo sapiens* brain. Understanding the *Homo sapiens* brain can be used as an approach to understanding the universe in which God lives.

Which brings us to *neuromodulation*. It is through neuromodulation that God talks to the human soul. The human soul is generally content, because it talks with God or His minions every night, and the human soul remembers these discussions. The *Homo sapiens* does not recognize or remember these dreams/conversations. The human being recognizes these conversations, but the information recognized is distorted to the point of being unreadable by the human mind and is therefore easily forgotten. It is the human being who feels the loss of God. A clear dream message would go unrecognized even if the human being could remember it, as there is significant temporal dissonance or dis-synchrony between heaven and earth. The isolated packages of information hidden in dreams arrive in weird, poorly predictable, asynchronous patterns.

Neuromodulation is how we can have three creatures inhabiting the same temporal body. Only one small group of clusters of axons is active at any given time in the ropy white-matter tract, but those that are active create a distinct active channel of consciousness. There are many channels. They are currently defined by the particular neurotransmitter that dominates, but a better classification is based upon looking at waves of action potentials and neurotransmitter release.

Neuromodulation is what is responsible for the human stream of consciousness defined by William James. This is the internal-versus-external origination of a series of thoughts, daydreams, and fantasies—sexual and otherwise, with old or new patterns of thought. Unless we focus, we run amok. Drugs change the focus. This change in focus may be enjoyable, and sometimes it can be helpful. But it can also be a distraction that can kill us.

The problem with secularism is that secularism denies the validity of all states of consciousness other than the so-called normal state of consciousness in which the so-called rational human being resides. This is a vital misunderstanding of the dominant subtype of the *Humanitas eternitas* larval instars that are currently alive on earth. The human being is not the *Homo sapiens*; you must either pull the veil down or lift it up and look underneath *before you can find the real human being.*

Secularism denies the validity of the human soul and greatly diminishes the potential of the human being. Secularism is the enemy of God. Secularism contains an evil that is dangerous to the human soul, but that is beyond the scope of this book.

There is no need for outrage while the human soul lives here on earth. We humans don't know what we are either fighting for or fighting against. Killing with high-explosive weaponry or nuclear detonations is wrong, and it is forbidden. If a person thinks his life here and now is bad, God can make sure that the next one is worse. Killing people with bombs is a sure way to go to hell. Suicide bombers are twice fools. Children can be talked into anything, and those who talk children into becoming suicide bombers are twice cursed. God has rules against this. Courting children for sex or bombs or abuse is proscribed. As for secularism, too much repression of the unconscious leads to a compulsive indulgence of the subconscious. Some seductions of the subconscious are dangerous and a threat to your sanity—so buyer, beware!

We have come a long way from the first parts of this chapter. There is too much information for a single reading, and perhaps too much for a single year of readings. It is not the usual presentation of neuroanatomy and human consciousness, and lots of things are left out. Everyone should know what a brain is, what is inside it, and how it works. Everyone should know what a mind is and what is included in that mind. Everyone should know the difference between the mind and the brain. Everyone should know that "stream of consciousness" is merely what you remember when scrolling through the channels of consciousness. Finally, everyone should realize that the ability to focus consciousness is the key to success. The ability to remember things at the periphery of your thoughts is an extremely good talent to have too, but that is a subjective talent. Memory, or the lack thereof, is the major tragedy of the human being. In fact, there are several minor tragedies.

Neuromodulation is more detailed and complex than what I have described. I have erred on the side of creating a few understandable thoughts rather than worrying about precision of detail.

10

ABORTION AND HOMOSEXUALITY

Because God prizes the human soul while having little or no regard for the *Homo sapiens* host animal, God has been content not to interfere with the activities and atrocities of human beings. God has always considered the *Homo sapiens* host animal to be a safe and dependable protective container in which to rear His children.

This is changing.

During the late nineteenth and all of the twentieth centuries, modern warfare and modern medicine prioritized the importance of the *Homo sapiens* over that of the human soul. It is as if the existence of the human soul has been actively denied by modern civilization. The result of this human miscalculation is that during the last one hundred years, more human souls have been injured, maimed, or killed than during the entire rest of human history. This makes God unhappy, and when God is unhappy, everyone is unhappy.

There is another aspect of humanity's disregard for the human soul. With the increase in cultural acceptance of abortion and homosexuality, the available numbers of host animals ready to receive their conjunction with the human soul are decreasing. This decrease in available host animals may or may not be a current problem, but when God has to anticipate a potential upcoming abortion, it becomes a logistical challenge, and it puts vulnerable instars at risk.

The human soul is attached to an earthly creature using the cat's cradle of active neurons within that host animal's brain stem and face. The host animal does not need to be mammalian; it just needs a central nervous system of moderate sophistication with the ability to engage in sleep behavior.

Implantation of the human soul occurs during the early midterm of the gestational period of the fetus during a host animal's pregnancy. The timing of this conjunction varies from specie to specie. In the *Homo sapiens*, it occurs after the twelfth week of gestation and before the nineteenth week. During the nineteenth week of a *Homo sapiens* pregnancy, the fetal glial cells appear to secrete serotonin at a rate and volume not seen during the remainder of that pregnancy, and these notably higher levels of serotonin bathe the fetal central nervous system for about one week.

This is called the serotonin spike, and this elevation of serotonin appears to solidify the gelatinous texture of the *Homo sapiens* fetal brain. This same spike serves to anesthetize the distressed, recently conjoined human soul. This anesthesia induces a prolonged coma-like sleep in the human soul for the remainder of that host animal's pregnancy, with the human soul only beginning to wake up when the fetal *Homo sapiens* respiratory nuclei begin to function. It is during that time of sedation that the human soul forgets all useful knowledge of its life before its current incarnation. While sedated, the human soul cannot be retrieved, as the retrieval mechanism requires that the human soul voluntarily exit its own entanglement with the host animal.

With the advent of modern medical techniques and the use of these techniques to perform abortions, the human soul encountered an unexpected risk to its health and safety, one that had not been present earlier in human history. As a general rule, the human soul does not die when its host animal dies. Unfortunately, due to the particular circumstances of vulnerability during a *Homo sapiens* pregnancy, a late-stage abortion can kill the human soul.

For these reasons, early abortion is acceptable to God when preformed prior to the twelfth week of gestation. Abortion is problematic and strongly discouraged during the twelfth through eighteenth weeks of gestation. Abortion is prohibited after the eighteenth week of gestation. The human soul can be retrieved with difficulty immediately after its implantation into the *Homo sapiens* fetus during the midterm of pregnancy, but it cannot be retrieved during the late term of pregnancy. The human soul is most vulnerable during late term gestation of its future host animal because it has been sedated. Sedation drastically increases the risk of death for the human soul because separation of the soul from the host animal requires the human soul to perform deliberate actions in the proper sequence. The soul cage is unlocked during the entire gestational period when the host animal shares the pregnancy with the human soul, as the unborn host animal does not yet have a functioning respiratory nucleus. The fact that the soul cage is unlocked during pregnancy does not make the separation process between fetal host animal and newly inserted human soul easy and it is during late gestation of the host animal that the human soul is most vulnerable and most easily killed.

Serotonin serves to hide the presence of heaven from the human soul during the entire lifetime of the host animal, but its function is most important to the newly inserted or conjoined human soul during the fetal period of its host animal. Serotonin is a big part, but not the only form of sedation affecting the human soul. In the adult *Homo sapiens*, low levels of serotonin allow the human soul to catch glimpses of heaven. But these glimpses of heaven reveal the vastly increased complexity and intensity of heaven relative to earth, and the glimpses of heaven appreciated by the human soul will generate a depressive response in the human being. This translates into a paradox: the human being becomes depressed with too direct an exposure to heaven. Too much serotonin in the host animal can decrease the dreaming experience for the conjoined human soul.

God's proscription against *Homo sapiens* homosexual activity is not directed at the act itself. Participation in homosexual activity is not a sin. God's proscription against homosexuality is simply due to this: God regards the *Homo sapiens* as breeding stock. Homosexuals acknowledge to themselves and others that they are "non-breeders." It is this non-breeding that is the sin against God. More *Homo sapiens* bodies are needed to carry the awaiting larvae of the *Humanitas eternitas* through their childhood, and *Homo sapiens* homosexual activity does not create these host animals. God judges people by evaluating their intent. The difference between a heterosexual couple adopting children and a homosexual couple adopting children is intent.

This raises the issue of God's difficulty matching available host animals to the current crop of human souls queued for their next incarnation. Not all *Homo sapiens* genotypes are compatible with all subtypes of *Humanitas eternitas*. Some combinations of subtypes of *Humanitas eternitas* and *Homo sapiens* result in disastrous phenotypes. Some people's lives roll easy, while others' lives do not. Some people, if they didn't have bad luck, would have no luck at all. Certain genetic profiles of *Homo sapiens* are not supportive of the immature instars, while other *Homo sapiens* genetic profiles have difficulty with mature instars. This is why it is important to maintain the genetic lineage of the *Homo sapiens* when a successful union of human soul and *Homo sapiens* is discovered.

One major difficulty with the cohabitation or conjunction of a human soul with a *Homo sapiens* is gender identification. Certain subtypes of *Humanitas eternitas* identify with either the male or female gender of the *Homo sapiens*, while others identify with neither or both. The more common subtypes of *Humanitas eternitas* are not as affected by gender mismatch with *Homo sapiens*, as are the rarer and more important subtypes of *Humanitas eternitas*. Having twenty-six *Humanitas eternitas* subtypes shoved into just two *Homo sapiens* genders is problematic. God judges this mismatch to be temporary and tolerable, and as the human soul needs an available series of host animals to facilitate a number of reincarnations before transcendence can be attempted, God assumes that instars will tolerate temporary gender mismatches.

But if a rare *Humanitas eternitas* subtype fails to produce *Homo sapiens* children, there may not be a host animal available for it when it comes time for the next reincarnation. Delayed reincarnation into another host animal carries a risk, and mismatches between human soul and *Homo sapiens* can lead to uncomfortable, unsuccessful, or even failed lives. If you want to go to heaven, you need to have future host animals available to you; therefore you need to have children. If one has no desire to go to heaven, the pressure is off, and there is no need to have children. Certain genetic profiles of the *Homo sapiens* are more important to God than others, just as certain genetic profiles of *Humanitas eternitas* are also more important than others. It is of particular note that racial subtypes of the *Homo sapiens*, which are so important here on earth, are not important to God.

Abortion and homosexuality are not trivial issues to God. God's main directive to His human children was this: Be fruitful and multiply. God did not direct His children to discover the true nature of the cosmos or of humanity, rather He told us to multiply. As much as human social mores change from century to century, some seemingly private, personal decisions are more rigidly discouraged than others. Abortion leading to the death of a human soul will be punished. The decision to be exclusively homosexual during this lifetime may lead God to let you stew in your own juices when it comes time for your next reincarnation.

11

TIME AND TIME²

I n the universe called earth, time is considered to be fundamental, meaning it cannot be subdivided into component parts. But in heaven, time is not fundamental. Time is the largest form of energy in the cosmos, and we here on earth are frozen out of it. Modern science can recognize the heavenly version of time, and we call it dark energy.

But when time spills over into our universe, it undergoes a phase change. It begins to fade away on a one-way ride to zero, traveling in a direction we cannot detect. Upon entering our universe, the universe of earth, time freezes in a liquid sort of way. In heaven, before time leaves the sixth dimension, it soars like an eagle, swooping and swirling, and it seems to be having a great time.

The Librarian whom our world knows as Sir Isaac Newton has transcended into heaven since his most famous sojourn on earth, and I am sure he loves it in heaven. Gottfried Leibniz was a Librarian too. They were both sent to deliver a series of messages to earth, and each succeeded in his own way. Their mission was to bring to the attention of humanity a mathematical way to measure and describe curves, circles, and spirals. Newton and Leibniz both brought calculus to earth; they both were librarians; they were both outsiders; and they were both trying and odd. When I think about it, it is pretty easy to guess the human identities of each of the Librarians up until a birth date of maybe 1945. After that it is hard for me to tell who is who. Librarians come in waves, usually two to six at a time, because there was a lot of attrition. If two Librarians succeeded at the same time, attempting the same goal, so much the better. Librarian success makes God happy.

At roughly five- to seven-hundred-year intervals, waves of Librarians have been sent to earth in large groups, meaning that as many as thirty individuals arrived and were all born in roughly the same birth year and in the same general geographic area. The first big group was huge and was subdivided into several large subgroups. Those groups were sent to various areas of the globe, mostly the Levant and Asia, about 4,500 years ago. They were instructed to address the issues of God and the nature of humanity. Several famous people were in those groups. Their message has been characterized as the "axial age"—humans on a journey through this world and into the next.

The next clusters of large groups were sent to the Levant at intervals of seven hundred years; they arrived 3,400, 2,000, and 1,400 years ago. The messages those groups delivered were also about the nature of God and humanity. These clusters were not as successful as God had planned. God realized that when the message He sent was about Himself, humanity did not take it well. Those Librarians were labeled as prophets, and they were often murdered before their messages were complete; or they became corrupted by public acclaim and judged themselves infallible, and their messages became distorted.

Thereafter, God changed strategies. His messages became more practical, with topics in mathematics, philosophy, physics, economics, human governance, and chemistry. The last three groups of Librarians were sent at more frequent intervals of about one hundred forty years, and most of those Librarians were sent to Europe. Time in heaven goes in circles or spirals or segmented cones, and these periodicities coincide with the closest temporal approaches between heaven and earth. These dates are important for a couple of reasons.

The last big cluster of Librarians, those sent about one hundred forty years ago, was supposed to pave the way to finding God, but their message was distorted, and wrong things were learned. Personally, I believe that Theodar Kaluza was the Librarian who was intended to discover heaven, but he misinterpreted the size of the fourth spatial dimension. Instead of discovering heaven, many Librarians in that cluster became distracted by relativity, quantum mechanics, and string theory. Some of the Librarians in that cluster were Max Planck, David Hilbert, and Albert Einstein. I believe their work suffered because Riemann died too early and Germany suffered political convulsions.

As a result of these problems, a huge signpost was missed. Bad things happened politically in Europe. Strange events occurred, and completely unexpected people came to power. And then worse things happened, and finally humanity acquired an atomic bomb. This was a catastrophic mistake. If God could do one thing, He would take the atomic bomb away from humanity. It is possible that no human souls will exist at the end of the next one hundred years because of this technology. Unfortunately, most of humanity is so caught up in its own public drama that no one is paying attention to this lethal weapon, a weapon that has fallen into the hands of children.

The only reason God put us down here on earth was to keep us out of trouble in heaven; and now, in this isolated, embargoed, boycotted world we call earth, an entire colony of human souls is on the verge of committing suicide. God may be bailing on humanity even now. God sent the Librarians to help humans define the shape of the manifold that we call the universe of earth. They were also sent to get the "timing" right on several reactions that occur both in heaven and on earth. Humans are never going to know which reactions God wants timed unless He tells us. But humans either cannot or will not listen to God; the entire relationship between God and humanity is in shambles.

Now, back to the topic of time and the manifold of space. Some may be asking, "What about black holes?" I know this was first on my list of concerns. Black holes aren't really holes at all; they are tears in the fabric of the universe. They are where the hard, parallel universe called earth spills into the softer universe called heaven. These are the places where you could try to look for heaven, but heaven will never be seen for real. We *Homo sapiens* do not have the sensory apparatus to detect heaven, and we do not know how to make the instruments that can. New and different instruments need to be developed in order for us to sense heaven, and we need some outside assistance to develop them.

One final thought about black holes: if a person fell into a black hole, he or she would freeze. There's the roar of all that stuff spilling and being sucked into heaven, and if you were to follow it in—you would freeze? I know; that does not seem right. Where does that stuff go? What happens after you freeze? I don't know.

Wormholes are different. Wormholes are useful. Using them is how you get from one place on earth to another remote place on earth by taking a shortcut through heaven. Wormholes are pretty common. They are located at some inflection points close to large gravitational masses, but they are also located close to the conjunctions of several lesser gravitational masses. You can go into wormholes and not die. Knowing and accepting where you end up is another matter. If you cannot come back from the places they take you, you are dead to earth but not to heaven.

The average human soul spends the better part of a thousand years on earth. The soul's life is fragmented, but it is continuous. Former lifetimes are not remembered; if they could be remembered, life here on earth would be better. If you think you have ten lifetimes to do something, you are right; but how do you know when you get to your tenth lifetime? The closer you get to that tenth lifetime, the more you'd better figure out what is truly important. God is looking over your shoulder every single night. God judges intent. Humility goes a long way in God's book, and God is vindictive. Dogmatic, cocksure idiots are almost as bad as pretentious, preening do-gooders. God has standards.

God also plays tricks on fanatics. Reincarnations are often coupled, and this coupling is referred to as "duplex lives." A European Christian in one life is often a Levant Muslim in the next, and vice versa. The same goes with all sorts of human conflicts: Palestinians and Israelis, Turks and Armenians, black people and white people in America, Russians and Ukrainians, Chinese and Vietnamese, etc. There are lots of items on that long list of duplex lives. Human folly used to be funny, but now the humor has a harder edge. You are what you hate. God may be the only one who gets the joke.

Democracy is not the ideal form of government, and centralized government is obscene. Plato has said this, and he too was a Librarian. Any government large enough to give you everything can take everything away, said Thomas Jefferson—another Librarian. Professional politicians are an obscenity. (This is me talking.) Bureaucracy is the antithesis of freedom. Only a few subtypes of *Humanitas eternitas* are judged upon their willingness and ability to follow directions. "Everything which is not forbidden is compulsory" is an appropriate slogan for only one of the twenty-six subtypes of *Humanitas eternitas*, yet that one subtype sticks its nose into everyone else's business.

Government does not have a responsibility to protect you—especially from yourself, which is the way of tyranny. Some pigs are more equal than others, said George Orwell—another Librarian. Orwell also said, "The hounds of hell are most terrifying when at a distance; once they have arrived, you are too busy surviving to care." Many, if not most, of the Librarians were not what the modern world calls politically correct, but the cost of not offending someone is a bumpy ride to hell. Librarians were outsiders, frequently pompous, antagonistic, and crude.

Well, this story deviated a long way from its supposed topic of time, probably because I know more about the topic of Librarians and the messages they were to deliver than I know about the topic of time.

12

Autism and Alzheimer's

The rapid arrival of these two diseases or conditions of humanity during the twentieth century reflects a major problem for both God and humanity. These seemingly different but obviously modern diseases or conditions of the *Homo sapiens* can be attributed to two things: modern warfare and modern medicine. Even as they appear to be conditions belonging to opposite poles of a *Homo sapiens* life span, they are manifestations of a single cause: an injured human soul.

When the host animal presents with either of these two new human conditions, the human soul must have sustained an injury. This injury usually occurred during the affected soul's previous incarnation. The most common injury to the human soul, which is expressed as either autism or Alzheimer's, is trauma.

Prior to talking about this particular form of physical injury to the human soul, we will talk about injuries in general to the *Homo sapiens*. Any trauma surgeon or nurse will tell you there is a huge spectrum of *Homo sapiens* injuries caused by trauma. This spectrum has many elements or variables.

The first variable is the amount of kinetic energy absorbed. That is, were you hit by a hammer or hit by a truck? The second is the speed with which that energy is delivered and absorbed. That is, you were hit by a truck, but was it traveling at five miles per hour or fifty miles per hour? The third variable involves the anatomical location of the injury. Were you hit in the head, chest, abdomen, pelvis, or leg? Fourth, what is the nature and direction of the force applied and absorbed, i.e., shearing, crushing, blasting, ripping, thermal, chemical, etc.? Was that force delivered from above, below, or behind? Was it glancing, left-sided, or right-sided, or was it delivered straight on, etc.?

Also, there are characteristic clusters of injury. Injuries come in groups, and if one particular anatomical spot is injured, another particular spot must be assessed for hidden injury. One particular set of injuries I have seen is called the "bordello injury." If someone jumps from the second story of a building and breaks his heel, you must also evaluate the lumbar spine for a compression fracture. There is a commonly seen cluster of injuries called the "seatbelt injury." These patterns of injury are well documented, and many textbooks have been written about these injuries.

These same principles of evaluation apply to injuries sustained by the human soul. It just takes a quantum increase in the amplitude and velocity of physical force applied to the *Homo sapiens* before the soul is affected. Modern medicine does not care about excessive force after a point. There is no difference to the *Homo sapiens* between being merely dead and being really, truly, most sincerely dead. For most of human history, and for most deaths occurring today, excessive force applied to the *Homo sapiens* brain stem was not an issue for God. Now it is.

Injuries to the human soul have a more limited presentation, and all injuries we recognize in the human soul occur to the soul at the same anatomical spot. This limits the spectrum of presentation, but it is more complicated to diagnose, because the injury presents via behavioral changes in a completely different *Homo sapiens* host animal.

I will concentrate on only one aspect of injury to the human soul, but there are others. The speed with which massive injuries resulting in death to the host animal arrive is the crux of this problem. The human soul will be affected if the death of its host animal occurs either too fast or, ironically, too slowly. This change in the velocity of *Homo sapiens* death is a phenomenon of the last part of the nineteenth and all of the twentieth centuries.

The type of earthly forces that can deliver a blow to the human soul is limited, and those forces did not exist until nineteenth- and twentieth-century human technology arrived. It takes a minimum of thirty years before the behavioral changes can be recognized within the next host animal. That is why injury to the human soul is a phenomenon of recent human history. Thus we have autism and Alzheimer's disease.

The human soul is tethered to the *Homo sapiens* host animal, and this tethering occurs around the neck and lower cranial vault of both animals. This tethering acts like a collar around the neck of the human soul and *Homo sapiens*. The brain stems and cranial nerves of both animals are superimposed upon one another and locked tight. This is called the *soul cage*. The anterior extracranial tracts of nerves are as important to the trap of the soul cage as is the desiccation of nerves within the brain stem. The key to the soul cage is the respiratory nuclei.

The brain stem is a protected area. Most forms of kinetic energy applied to the *Homo sapiens* will not be absorbed by the brain stem, with one exception: high explosives. The nature of a high explosive is that it creates a shock wave of energy that arrives at a velocity greater than ten thousand feet per second, delivering an intense volume of energy over an extraordinarily short period of time. This shock wave shears the bond between human soul and *Homo sapiens*, injuring or killing one, while killing or breaking the other into pieces.

Why does this speed of death matter? Because the speed of extraction of the human soul exiting the *Homo sapiens* is rate limited. It takes time. First, the soul cage must be unlocked; second, the human soul must voluntarily initiate the extraction process; and third, the disentanglement is not instantaneous. It is similar to taking off a pair of boots. The entire process requires five to ten minutes at best and usually takes several hours.

Traditional forms of death for the *Homo sapiens* have allowed this extraction to happen without constraint, but with the introduction of high explosives into modern warfare, high-speed, highly kinetic energy causes injuries resulting in instantaneous death to the *Homo sapiens* and nonfatal injuries to the human soul. The consequences begin to be recognized in the behavior of that human soul's next host animal during that soul's next reincarnation.

There are two modes of presentation. One occurs early in life and affects the host animal's behavior for its entire life, and the other expresses itself as the human soul collapsing somewhat before the end of the next host animal's life. When I say that the soul collapses, I mean that it has not and cannot escape the soul cage. It stays where it was put, but it pulls away from interactions with both its host animal and its environment. Humanity calls the same disease by two different names: Alzheimer's and autism. Neither of these presentations is recognized by modern medicine as being the same disease. However, modern medicine recognizes that these are both newly arrived, and it will concede that both are poorly understood.

Let's come back to the velocity of death. Another problem facing the human soul is the forced, abnormal prolongation of a *Homo sapiens* life. This prolongation is usually done with medical respirators, but it is not limited to that form of medical treatment. However, I will concentrate on the respiratory lock. If there is a complete shutdown of the host animal's respiratory nuclei, the soul cage becomes unlocked. The unlocking of the soul cage means that the human soul has been given a signal that the time has come to return home to Valhalla. Initial failure of the respiratory nuclei will open the lock, but the medical respirator will relock it.

How quickly the human soul responds to this release signal depends on how ready it is to leave that host animal when the signal arrives. The application of the respirator to the otherwise dying or dead *Homo sapiens* relocks the released lock after the signal has been sent. The soul realizes that it has become trapped within an otherwise dead host animal. Functionally, this is a drowning. When respirators are used to save a *Homo sapiens* life, there is a time limit of roughly forty-eight hours. After that, the human soul begins to slowly die. Beyond seven days of confinement, the human soul is almost certainly dead.

The human soul, who would otherwise have a life span approaching one hundred thousand years, with a thousand years or more of that spent as instars, now has seven days to live. There is something tragic about ruining a one-hundred-thousand-year lifetime because seven days are spent trying to save what is essentially an already dead *Homo sapiens*.

The needs of the human soul are in direct opposition to the activities of modern warfare and modern medicine. High-explosive injury or traumatic brain injury in one *Homo sapiens* can be detected either in the early development of the next host animal as autism, or later as Alzheimer's disease.

If a human soul is normal, it is inserted into the next host animal, on average, twenty-seven years after the death of the previous host animal. Thus, on average, a host animal killed during World War I would be reincarnated sometime after 1940. Those killed in World War II would have been reincarnated after 1970. Those killed in the Korean War would have been reincarnated after 1980, and those killed in Vietnam would have been reincarnated sometime after 1995. Those human souls whose host animals were killed by bullets, napalm, or chemicals would not have been affected by this high-velocity death.

Those human souls whose host animals were killed in high-explosive events resulting in relative disintegration of the host animal's body would be dead. The human souls who are most severely affected by the velocity of the previous host animal's death are probably kept longer in Valhalla than is typical. This delay between cause and effect is the reason that autism and Alzheimer's disease have had a dramatic increase during the last years of the twentieth century.

High explosives and nuclear detonation will totally annihilate the human soul, as it fractures the *Homo sapiens* into pieces or small bits of dust. If the body of a host animal can't be found, the human soul is dead. As far as God is concerned, this makes the use of high explosives and nuclear detonations verboten. If a soldier, general, or politician has killed or caused to be killed any human soul by the use of high explosives or nuclear detonations, that soldier, general, or politician will be punished by God. This is one of the messages I have been told to deliver: "Stop the current use of high-explosive weaponry in human warfare." It does not, or should not, take a rocket scientist to recognize the danger to the human soul from modern warfare.

13

No One Wants to Be a Prophet

Modern secular society is convinced that God—if He, She, or It exists—is not a he, a she, or an it. Secularists believe that if a God exists, it has no anthropomorphic characteristics at all. God—perhaps with a lowercase *G*—is merely the compilation of the laws of physics and perhaps psychology, nothing more. The only prophets I have ever encountered were on a soapbox in London and near a shooting gallery in a back alley of the Mission district in San Francisco, the latter being a person I had the misfortune to meet while shopping for a rug.

The religious concept of God proposed by the religions of Abraham—Judaism, Christianity, and Islam—as a caring, judging, anthropomorphic entity worthy of devotion cannot be reconciled with the other criteria for God, especially His omnipotence and omniscience. A prophet who has seen God, who makes predictions about the future, and who claims to speak for God is obviously crazy, deluded, or dangerous. The prophet is someone to be avoided. No one wants to be a prophet, particularly in an age without God.

Prophets should also be ignored. If one listens to a prophet, one could end up in a cult, isolated from society and quite possibly ending one's life by drinking poisoned Kool-Aid. I don't even like listening to missionaries from Christian churches, and I am familiar with the canon from which they teach. Prophets claim too much. No one wants to be a prophet, particularly in an age without God.

I spent much of my life intermittently carrying a childhood memory that grew more and more indistinct and unbelievable as I aged. I wrote it off as an early childhood fantasy that could be ignored. But then I had an overwhelming religious experience that changed my entire outlook on life. What would a secularist do if something obviously more powerful than human, more compelling than any other experienced event, suddenly entered his life? After much consideration would he conclude that this event could only be a religious experience, an encounter with the holy? What if the presence he thought to be divine asked him to do something—something he did not want to do?

It took me several years to answer this question, and this is my answer: if someone honestly believes that God has asked/told him to do something, he had damned well better do it. In the end it is a simple decision, but it is an unbelievably complex decision to make.

Thus I have created a body of work that was not dictated to me in a prepackaged form by some ethereal angel, and no muse sat upon my shoulder. Rather, I have been exposed to a divine presence that flooded me with thoughts, ideas, and knowledge I had never otherwise been exposed to. That presence then enjoined me to publicly express memories of my bizarre experience, one that requires understanding and the describing of a complex and elaborate relationship between two parallel universes. I was told to describe something I have never seen and to make pronouncements I would not otherwise believe. I have been assigned to use words to define that for which there are no words. And God gave me no opportunity to review my memories with a higher authority.

This is a true test of faith. I have become a proponent for a belief system completely at odds with all current ideas of modern civilization, the current paradigms of both East and West. Why should anyone speak for God? Why would anyone voluntarily step into that morass? Only the deluded, psychotic, or socially inept would do so. Only fools go in—which may be me, but I try to hide it.

But … I believe I encountered a divine entity, and He (in my case I thought this divine entity was male) asked me to publicly talk about the encounter, an encounter that occurred in two parts. One part occurred on the day before I was to be inserted into the *Homo sapiens* body I now inhabit. I remember sometime later, in kindergarten, asking other kids my age about their earliest memories, and no one had memories like mine. My original memory was something I had overcome by late childhood. It was mostly gone by age ten and was generally ignored until I had my second, more traditional religious experience at the age of fifty-three.

That second part of my encounter was probably precipitated by uncontrolled diabetes. I speculate that this entire book—which you, the reader, are currently reading and judging—is an attempt to prove that I am not crazy. A psychiatrist has told me that I am bipolar and that these writings I have worked on for a decade are so much rubbish, something to be put away.

I have thought about this a great deal. I believe that the current meme about prophets is wrong. I have come to believe that there is a spectrum of prophets from lesser to greater, some predicting the future, and others declaring clarifications of certain fine points of Scripture. Most of these prophets are harmless, but they also speak in code. I have come to believe that they should not be ignored.

There are a great many lesser prophets; perhaps as many as two or three percent of people could be lesser prophets if they had the self-confidence to go public, but where does prophecy end and opinion begin? Being a greater prophet is another story; there is true pathology there. I have been called to go forth and publicly present this theory of life, this new hermeneutic interpretation of the canon of Abraham and the Pentateuch, this reclamation of the entire works of Descartes, this reiteration of Kant. I must speak the unspeakable to an age without God.

I don't have the public presence to talk to even thirty people, but I have been called. I still do not have the self-confidence to go out in public with conflicting data and tangle with politically correct thoughts, but I am doing it. I'm not doing it out of narcissism or overt psychosis; I have grown used to being invisible. I sincerely believe that I can become essentially invisible, almost at will. People will not notice me, even if I am looking at them and standing in their way. I think it is a function of intuition, even if calling it that is counterintuitive. I sometimes think I can force someone not to notice me. I often notice four-legged animals before other people do, even before dogs can sense a foreign presence. When living on the edge of the wilderness as I do, that is a skill that comes in handy.

I have two closely related talents that make me unique, and perhaps these traits or talents define the Librarian. I have marked talents in both intuition and empathy. These are not the same, although they are often conflated. Intuition says, "I know something, or several somethings, about someone or some situation that I have no possible reason to know." Empathy is sharing emotions and emotional thoughts with someone, usually without the other person's awareness that this sharing is being done. This often leads to greater understanding of relationships and situations than is advisable for either me or the other.

Neither of these talents or traits is publicly displayed. They are a burden, and they are hard to carry. I seek shelter in the rain. I go outside into the woods and cut trees. I am talking about these traits because I have them and yet can barely control them. In the long run, I do not believe I have benefited from having them, but I believe they are part of being a Librarian. I do not think either trait is connected to my religious experiences, but I could be wrong. Intuition does not have to involve other people or even living creatures at all. Empathy does not have to involve humans, but the subject of your empathetic probe must be alive.

What do I mean by *intuition*? I have had no formal training in how to be intuitive. Intuition is hard to define, but it colors everything I do. I can get intuitive "strikes" while casually walking through a department store. People tend to decrease their psychic defenses when in a crowd. But those insights and the knowledge I gain from strangers will fade almost as fast as I encounter the next person. Still, if I know the person from whom I receive intuitive information, I can put these small glimpses of insight into a larger context, and they become a powerful tool. But too frequently in my youth, intuition provided more power than I knew how to use. I used it as a weapon. I fought dirty.

I realize that my insights into other people's souls have frightened those with whom I was in competition. I can read people's thoughts by reading their emotions. If I get the intuitive flash, I can tell what is going to happen. If I get the empathetic flash, I can tell motive instantly. If there is conflict in a group of people around the table, I can tell who is thinking what—for almost everyone in the room. I have to block myself from doing it.

Intuition is a two-edged sword. As a youth, I could not control it, so I had to suppress it. Most "intuitives" do not know that other people do not share this skill or talent. Many intuitives do not "get it"; they are confused by the discrepancy between that which they know to be true and that which others insist is true. I call these intuitives "intuitards." But I believe intuition can be taught, and I believe there is an entire system of rules for using it. I have not been taught the rules, but I think I know what they should be.

I want to reiterate some thoughts, and perhaps I will phrase them differently from before. I want to speak of Valhalla and some thoughts I associate with it. The average time a human soul spends resting and recuperating between human entanglements in Valhalla is approximately twenty-seven years. It can be as few as six years or as many as ninety years, and the mean is thirty years. This time around, they gave me seven weeks between host animals. Then, to make things worse, they conjoined me to a fetus at about twenty weeks' gestation, just *after* the serotonin spike, which meant that I was not sedated for the remaining twenty weeks of my mother's pregnancy. I lacked sedation at a time intended to provide respite for the human soul, but for me it was a time of torture and fear.

I had too many memories of Valhalla as an infant. I was a colicky baby. I did not thrive for the first twelve weeks. I lost almost three pounds out of seven and almost died in the first few months of life. This is probably why God does not put human souls into *Homo sapiens* fetuses after eighteen weeks of gestation. The cost of getting a glimpse behind the cover that hides our past is expensive. I don't think this experience of remembering the past has anything to do with my talents with intuition and empathy. This glimpse behind the curtain is what is driving my need to write and publish this experience, because this is what I promised to articulate when I remembered.

But it took a second religious experience—a more traditional experience similar to those described in William James's book, *The Varieties of Religious Experience*—to get me to write this book.

My second religious experience had an abrupt onset. I was listening to one of the Teaching Company's lectures on tape, "The History of

Science in the Twentieth Century," while driving home from work in the fall of 2005, when, in close conjunction, the professor addressed two issues: the speed of light, and the amount of our cosmos that is hidden by dark energy and dark matter. And suddenly I *knew* where and what heaven is. With that insight came a cascade—more of a torrent—of knowledge and information.

I was engulfed. It was like standing next to the outflow pipes of the hydroelectric plant at Bonneville Dam with a teacup, trying to collect as much of the water as I could. I got more than I expected, but I got wet. The initial rush lasted about eight hours; the faucet was open for a week. I was consumed with trying to collect and remember as much of this data as I could. There were no external restrictions on what I sought, and I had to let many interesting topics slide by for lack of time, personal endurance, and understanding.

None of the information and insights I derived seemed absurd, ridiculous, or fanciful at the time, yet the volume of knowledge to which I was exposed made me realize how pathetic human knowledge is when compared to the cosmos. That which I could not understand humbled me. I was further humbled by how small a part the human plays in the cosmos. But the human has a unique and important role, and the irony is that we humans have virtually no idea what that role is. The clearest message I received was that the human being has conflated humanity with the *Homo sapiens*.

I suddenly became a dreadful dualist and a proponent of the axial theory of human life. I suddenly knew—and by this I mean a justified, true belief—that the canon of religious literature belonging to the religions of Abraham carry the truth, but not in the literal sense. The canon was dictated and articulated by heavenly creatures who knew much about space and nothing about the earthly concept of time, while this same canon was transcribed by unsophisticated humans who understood the earthly concept of time but nothing about the heavenly concept of space.

Also, I realized that the current interpretation of the canon by ethical monotheists is confused and misinformed as to the true nature of the audience. The canon was intended to inform and instruct the human soul on how to live as a human; it was not intended for the *Homo sapiens*. Again, mankind is confused as to who we really are. The Bible, particularly the Pentateuch, is mostly a series of stories instructing the human soul as to how to live life as a human being. An example of this difference is this: *Homo sapiens* did not engage in either lying or betrayal until it became infected with the human soul. Deception—including self-deception—is integral to the human being. It is a feature and not a bug. No one has any grievance or entitlement to become self-righteous about.

In anticipation of criticism, I will address the issue of cognitive distortions. Secularists will nullify many of my statements and arguments as examples of poor mental hygiene. By relying strictly upon rational, normal consciousness as the sole standard by which everything else is judged, most of my stories can be dismissed as containing multiple, significant, cognitive distortions. Clearly, I have made claims about magical thinking, mind reading, and fortune-telling that are at odds with secular thought.

Overgeneralization, emotional reasoning, and even catastrophizing are also claims that could be laid at my feet. My response to those criticisms may be weak, but it is this: the standards and jargon of one paradigm cannot be used against individual components of another paradigm, as it is much like comparing apples to oranges. A new paradigm must be evaluated in its totality by comparing it to reality using its own internal logic and reasoning. Comparing one paradigm with another will reveal conflicting truths, but it will not reveal the preeminence of one paradigm over another.

There is one final problem with being a prophet. They have no peers. No one is there to bounce ideas off of. There is no one to whom a prophet can say, "I am confused about this detail ..." Any presentation of any portion of the prophecies is met with silence, careful questioning, or outright rejection and ridicule. No one provides the prophet with helpful hints. The nature of a religious experience is such that the prophet cannot request a second or third presentation of the event for his or her review.

No one wants to be a prophet. As much as a person may desire to be one of the chosen ones, as much as a person may wish to carry a message or a warning from God, as much as a person may want to receive a glimpse into the future, being selected to be a prophet is not so much a blessing as it is a curse.

Being a prophet is very much in keeping with the Celtic notion of carrying a giese, with one exception: a giese brings with it the requirement of voluntary acceptance of an obligation. The word "giese" is an uncommon and infrequently translated concept of a covenant between a person and God which was created by the druids. That commitment, that covenant, was accepted by the Celtic traditions and language but has not made the transition into English.

The prophet—as opposed to the giesist—is selected without regard to his or her personal acceptance or rejection of a contract with God. With selection comes obligation; the prophet has a duty and a responsibility to get his message right. And yet the prophet is allowed just one pass at the brass ring. If the giesist accepts this same obligation, he/she is given unlimited attempts to get the message right, with only one restriction; there is only one attempt from each host animal. The line between being a true prophet and a false prophet is narrow, and only God will know if the prophet got it right. The reader may reject my efforts on many levels, but my audience is God, and it is through Him that I will be judged. Not everyone who comes to earth is also given homework, I was given homework because I accepted the giese. This book is the completion of my homework assignment from God.

14

TALKING TO GOD

In order to talk with God, you must first know yourself.

Normal human consciousness is anything but normal to the human being. The myth that a human is strictly the *Homo sapiens* is a secular delusion created as a second-order derivative or by-product of the belief that God is dead. It is one of several myths, such as a belief in communism that needs to die.

One reason for this confusion between human being and *Homo sapiens* is our failure to recognize how much of our normal waking hours are spent in non-normal states of consciousness. Why are we unaware of how long we are absent from a normal, conscious focus during any given hour? How much of our time, in private and in public, is not spent focused upon what we are supposed to be doing? We will never know unless we look. The *Homo sapiens* does not have instant access to recall the contents of certain intermediate or short-term memory banks, which are available for normal consciousness's neuromodulatory channels, so many daydreams are recorded but cannot be consciously replayed.

Most memory banks used for instantaneous, conscious recall are available only to those neuromodulatory (NM) channels we call normal consciousness. Other NM channels do not have short-term memory banks. This scrambling back and forth between different NM channels is like surfing between five or six channels on TV, jumping channels by making conscious decisions about which button to push. The focal point from which we are directed to focus our concentration or attention is the thing that controls the percentage of time we spend on the channels of normal human consciousness, but there is limited voluntary control over which channel we focus upon.

There are gradations of consciousness and a maximum level of consciousness, which we sometimes achieve when taking standardized tests. Then there is the more relaxed level of consciousness that occurs in a darkened classroom at 2:30 in the afternoon. And then there is outright daydreaming, and these NM channels are non-normal. There are fantasy NM channels, sexual fantasy NM channels, and even guilt channels on the NM radio dial. We could go on endlessly.

Generally, adult *Homo sapiens* do not spend much time during normal working hours in non-normal channels, but we spend more time there than we think. On each working day our NM stay is short—perhaps fifteen to forty-five seconds—and then we move on into a more normal channel. But we may go into NM channels fifty or sixty times an hour.

After hours—or when we are relaxing with a particularly interesting daydream or a persistent fantasy or are indulging in mild recreational drugs—we can spend many minutes, sometimes hours, on non-normal NM channels. Sometimes this time spent elsewhere is not recalled immediately upon returning to a normal channel. This is so common that there is a name for it: "lost in thought."

It could be argued that the activities primarily devoted to being a *Homo sapiens* are those preformed during normal consciousness or on most normal-consciousness channels. But the activities of the human soul are preformed on non-normal NM channels. The activities of the human being are preformed on a mixture of normal and non-normal channels, and the patterns of usage and range of channels available vary greatly from person to person.

We can step away for a moment and look at those three divisions of consciousness: the normal conscious, the non-normal conscious (which could also be called the subconscious), and the unconscious. The paradigm that secularists accept argues that the only valid thoughts that a human thinks occur in the rational brain on the normal-consciousness NM channels. They further think that that which occurs on non-normal consciousness NM channels is pathology. They further think that that which occurs exclusively on non-normal consciousness NM channels is a random discharge of nerves, a resetting process. Thus, by this belief, secularists rob themselves of two thirds of the available NM channels. Their refusal to watch other NM channels, the ones without a connection to normal consciousness, eliminates the sensory perceptions associated with those different NM channels and negates any possible contribution from those NM channels to the human being's perception of reality. This does not mean that secularists are unable to tap into creative channels of thought and emotion, but in order to do so, they must step out of thought processes or NM channels in the normal consciousness sub-set and employ the channels dedicated to sub-conscious or even unconscious mentation.

There is an important book called *The Structure of Scientific Revolutions* by Thomas Kuhn. In it he describes two ways that normal science and revolutionary science can be performed. Normal science is preformed on normal-consciousness NM channels, and I am saying that revolutionary science is performed on non-normal NM channels. It is actually more complicated than that. Sensory perceptions, the concept of truth, moral values, and more—all vary depending upon which channel you are on. The length of time spent upon certain NM channels and which other NM channels you habituate will affect the you that is you. Creativity, successful artistry, and revolutionary science are performed on the margins of normal consciousness with a distinct quantum increase in contribution from the non-normal channels. This is where the intuitives operate. The empaths work here too, just on different NM channels.

Normal-consciousness NM channels result in more ridged, concrete thinking. There are many common patterns of NM channel use.

Current NM channels are defined and categorized by their neurotransmitters, but this is an incomplete characterization, as each system of nerves driven by a single specific neurotransmitter does not work alone. These nerves work in combination with nerves operating from other neurotransmitters, and these nerves work in clusters of specific, but as yet unrecognized, ratios of neurotransmitter systems of neurons at any given moment.

The well-known neurotransmitters—such as serotonin, acetylcholine, dopamine, norepinephrine, and gamma amino butyric acid—each cause different perceptions, analyses, and behaviors. There are dozens of neuromodulatory channels that fall under the blanket of normal consciousness, while other combinations do not. Neurotropic drugs—cocaine, cannabinoids, opioids, and amphetamines—are also neurotransmitters. That is why they have psychotropic affects and why they affect a person's perception of life. The habituative nature of these chemicals may reflect the human soul's desire to exist in a state of non-normal human consciousness, to linger on non-normal NM channels.

The specifics of which clusters of neuropathways and which neurotransmitters cause which NM channels are currently unknown. One thing can be said with certainty: normal human consciousness is the mental state of consciousness, the cluster of operative NM channels, and it is completely unaware of God.

How many of these conscious NM channels go unremembered or partially remembered, and how many of these NM channels can be voluntarily accessed even if they are poorly remembered? How many of the poorly remembered or not remembered NM channels must be accessed on a daily basis? What does the sequence of scrolled-through NM channels tell about a person?

Dreams are necessary for survival of the *Homo sapiens*, but which other non-normal consciousness NM channels are equally necessary? The conscious state one enters while having a sexual encounter is a non-normal state of consciousness. It could be argued that at certain times of life there is a compulsion to enter that non-normal state of consciousness on a regular basis. Understanding the rhythms of these recurrent non-normal states of consciousness may be a clue to understanding this vital aspect of human behavior.

Sorting through and understanding what these various states of human consciousness mean, and learning which NM channel is associated with which state of consciousness, are the key to finding a way for humans to actually talk to God.

First, we must find a way for humans to remember the unremembered. Second, we must unravel the language of each non-normal state of consciousness. And third, we must trust those who claim to be talented enough to interpret the data. The route to using this *Homo sapiens* dream instrument to explore the cosmos is through the analysis of dreams. Dreams can be counted and measured, and they occur with great and predictable regularity. If dreams are the communication channels by which we talk to God, certain stereotypical patterns of communication should be detectable.

There is probably no Rosetta stone for dreams, but we will not know unless we look for it. If we are looking for a conversation, that will guide our search. We must unravel the languages used in each dream sequence, create a transcript of the various dreams, and then learn to control our side of the conversation. Remember, we are looking for someone who wants to be found, but we are not looking for a mirror. Once we have found these components, we should find some predictable response from God, such as, "Welcome! I am glad you have found me."

Once we have gotten that far, once we suspect that we might be talking to God, then we can set traps to ensure that we are not talking with ourselves.

15

CONCLUSION

We have come to the end of this series of stories. I have not been writing a textbook. I have been writing an appeal to both the conscious self and the subconscious self. The unconscious self will find out later. But my appeal to these non-normal NM channels in your head cannot be made directly. I don't think what I'm trying to do can be done. I'm trying to change a paradigm. This is David-and-Goliath stuff. This is small-rudder-steering-big-ships stuff. I am tilting at windmills—yes, that is more like it.

What was asked of me was simple on the face of it. *Just publicly speak about as much of this place as you can remember.* I have distinct memories of a specific place, Valhalla. These are vivid flashes of specific moments in the weeks before I was entwined with my current *Homo sapiens* host animal during an abnormally late stage of the pregnancy in which I was the fetus. It was this late insertion, later than twenty weeks, that allowed some memories to be retained. None of us are *tabula rasa*; John Locke was wrong. A couple of the Librarians really got their assignments wrong. Jean-Jacques Rousseau was another.

It is not that we are a blank slate when we are born; it is just that the human cannot articulate, recognize, and produce on command all the memories we possess. In my case, the memories were retained long enough because I did not experience that fetal bath in serotonin. I kept those memories long enough to find new places to store them more permanently. If I were like everyone else, I would not have these memories. The question is: am I crazy or am I called? I have these memories. I have convinced myself that they are real, and I have found a way to put them into context. The idea that this could be a well-developed psychosis is unsettling.

But my memory is conflicted, because it involves a divine person whom I have conflated with God. Clearly, this is delusional. I am an angry, arrogant, well-educated, former professional who does not attend church, even though I was educated in part by Jesuits. I have found a new hermeneutics, which I deem to be of vital necessity in this day and age. I have been exposed to Scriptures, to the Pentateuch, and to the canon of the religions of Abraham, and I accept them. I accept the Scriptures for what they are: attempts by unsophisticated men using inadequate languages to describe the indescribable.

Scripture is neither an accurate nor true reflection of God's Word. All Scripture comes from a divine inspiration, but all Scripture must be filtered through a human being's mind. That mind must provide context, and *the act of providing context* distorts the truth. But the canon is close to truth, and that is just one amazing thing about it. The process of turning dreams or religious experiences into cogent, tangible words on a piece of paper is remarkable in its accuracy—but the results need reinterpretation.

In a new age of man, one with new requirements and responsibilities from God, a new hermeneutic or interpretation of Scripture is needed. With no one else to provide one, I had to fall upon my sword and provide one. I have endured the pangs of solitude but have received riches there. These riches are what this poor offering is intended to be.

A new hermeneutic: that is what this is. This is an offering, an approximation of the truth. This offering describes a very particular cosmos divided into two well-known, parallel universes and then suggests that a true understanding of the cosmos is not to be gained through current astronomy. Rather, this paradigm, this hermeneutic, suggests that the *Homo sapiens* itself serves as the antenna or telescope used by the human being, and this instrument is intended to probe the parallel universe we call heaven.

I admit that the conditions as described are unlikely, but I submit that they are true. Sincerity is no barometer of truth, but justified true belief is knowledge. If I understood the language of mathematics, much of what I have described about physics and astronomy would be easier to define, but I needed an understanding of the *Homo sapiens*, and that required my current host animal's pursuit of a medical career. I was not suited to become a physician; I had too much empathy. I had to forcibly hide or suppress the empathy I felt, which frequently caused people to think I had none at all.

Also, I was given too many empathetic and intuitive skills, and my ability to overhear fragments of thoughts and emotions emanating from other people was a dreadful burden that I could not carry for long. Being privy to too many other people's emotions caused me to seek refuge in solitude. I seek shelter in the rain. I have become a woodsman.

My point, at the end of all this rambling, wandering perusal of half-painted portraits, is this: I met someone important who asked me to publicly state whatever memories I could remember about the time I spent just before my birth during that short transition period between my last two human lives in the place I call Valhalla.

I remembered this request, and I have carried this memory in some form since birth, but for the vast majority of my life, I could not figure out how to describe my experience and those memories. Those words were provided to me as a by-product of a singularly intense religious experience similar to those described by William James. I experienced a weeklong, manic rush of ideas, thoughts, and understanding. I kept copious notes. I was given the keys to the cosmos; any question I wanted to ask would be answered. It was an event beyond my expectations or understanding. I could not retain most of what was given to me. It was like standing in front of the exit pipes of the hydroelectric turbines of Bonneville Dam with a teaspoon in my hands.

There are a few generalities I remember from my tour of the cosmos. Humanity understands less than 10 percent of all that is knowable about the cosmos. It is worse than that; there are several fundamental facts about our own universe of which we are unaware, and it is very much to our own discredit that we have not discovered their importance and accepted those memes. Beyond that, about two thirds of all the knowledge in the cosmos is unavailable to us. Humanity does not even know the contours of the stage upon which our lives are set. Humanity has been intentionally isolated. It is a test, and we are failing, proving that we need isolation. Earth is not a prison, although it feels like one. It is more a day care center with no adult supervision.

Humanity has not performed well. God is displeased. He is of two minds: pull out the human souls who can still be saved, or try to reach out to humanity through the only voice He currently has available, the voice of a prophet.

God's most important message is this: the *Homo sapiens* is not the human being. The human soul in combination with the *Homo sapiens* is the human being. Modern secular society denies the existence of the human soul, thereby denying the essence of humanity. Another aspect of the problem God has with secularism is that secularism denies the importance of nonrational thought in the human. God regards nonrational human thought and the non-normal states of human consciousness to be vital.

God's equally important message is this: humanity must give up its biggest weapon, the nuclear bomb. But God's full message is even worse for humanity: we must also give up the high explosives used in conventional warfare. Humanity simply does not have the maturity to handle these weapons. There is an ancient saying that we have ignored for the last century: "Beware of high-grade fires."

Low-velocity *Homo sapiens* death—even if agonizing and painful, even if coming via nerve gas, smallpox, bullets, or Ebola—is a *Homo sapiens* death that the human soul will survive. There is one important exception regarding low-velocity death, and it reflects upon modern secular technology. The too-slow death of a *Homo sapiens*—a death resulting from modern medicine keeping the *Homo sapiens* alive at the expense of the human soul—must be avoided. These two kinds of death of a host animal, either too fast or too slow, create autism and Alzheimer's in the next reincarnation. The history of man is a twisted and intertwined series of tales of the same souls living in different bodies over the period of one thousand years. Friends, foes, things you hate and things you love, friends and battles won and lost—if only we knew the rules …

God holds little hope that even this seemingly simple request—a request to change the manner in which host animals die—can be understood and accepted by modern humanity. Too much secular influence is poorly balanced by too much religious fanaticism in today's world. It certainly will not be politically correct to pull a respirator at forty-eight hours in every case, and it will be virtually impossible to take bombs away from generals.

The use of medical ventilators provides life for the *Homo sapiens*, while it kills or maims the human soul. Nuclear detonation will instantly kill the human soul as it vaporizes the *Homo sapiens*. High-explosive detonations will either kill or maim the human soul as it kills the *Homo sapiens*. If humanity indulges its most primitive and immature impulses by engaging in a nuclear war, no matter what the reason, then the best and the brightest of human souls will be destroyed. The perpetrator and all active participants in a nuclear war will be punished forever, and that punishment will be far worse than death.

Beyond that injunction, God sincerely wishes to establish communication with His children, but that contact must be initiated by humanity, and God fears that it is unlikely to be established in time. Humanity does not know where to look for God. Humanity does not know which instrument to use in order to find God. And finally, humanity may not be mature enough to talk to God.

Before World War I, God was confident that He would see each of us again during our next return to Valhalla. By the end of the World War II, that was no longer the case. Therefore, a prophet was needed, and one has been sent. God has sent me here to tell you this: "Good bye."

ABOUT THE AUTHOR

The author was living a normal secular life as a practicing physician when, in the autumn of 2005, he endured a weeklong epiphany: a religious experience that was personally compelling and caused him to change the direction of his life. It took the author ten years to assimilate the information he received during that single week.

The author did not want to write this book. Indeed, he does not know if all of the details are correct, even though the intent is clear. The author was asked by a divine entity to make this knowledge public. The author was confronted with a simple choice: ignore the experience, turn his back on God, and continue to live a normal life—or write it down and endure the slings and arrows of outrage and ridicule.

The author lives among the trees with his wife, five dogs, two horses, a large bird, and many motorized off-road vehicles along the banks of a beautiful year-round creek at the edge of BLM and National Forest land in Southern Oregon. It could be said he lives on the margins of society.

ABOUT THE BOOK

The human soul is the forgotten piece of the puzzle of humanity. One human soul was awakened early while recently returned to Valhalla between reincarnations, and he was intentionally placed into the late-term pregnancy of a new host animal for an exceptionally quick return to earth. God instructed him to tell humanity as much as he could remember about the mechanics of how God tends the human soul prior to that soul's entering heaven. The resulting book provided a new way to interpret the Scriptures, for there was one final message God wanted this impromptu prophet to deliver to mankind.

Lightning Source UK Ltd.
Milton Keynes UK
UKOW02f1830081016

284779UK00001B/96/P